Balanchine's Dancing Cowboy

Dear Laura,

Hope you enjoy this saga of a special friendship. So important to all of us. Our friendship with you & Howard enriches us greatly!

Love, Emily

Balanchine's Dancing Cowboy

Frank Ohman and Emily Berkowitz

ePUBit • New York City

ISBN - 10: 0988931869

ISBN - 13: 978-0988931862

Published 2013 by ePUBit

167 East 82nd Street

New York, New York 10028

Photographs on front cover, page 102, and page 188 courtesy of the Martha Swope Foundation.

DEDICATIONS

This book is lovingly dedicated to those who meant and mean the most to me and taught me much:

My grandmother, Stella Childs Harsan
My mother, Irene Ohman Phillips
George Balanchine
My son, Johan

— FRANK OHMAN

For my greatest champions, my husband, Jay, and my son, Justin, for their support and encouragement of this project. You have my heart, forever.

For my parents, Anne and Herb Goldstein, for introducing me to the glorious world of the arts.

For my sister, Marjorie Goldstein, for insisting we get subscriptions to the NYCB. I love you.

For my friends and newest family member, Jessica, I am eternally grateful to you for being a vital part of, and enriching, my life.

For Larry Abelove, for teaching me anything is possible.

For my co-author and friend, Frank Ohman, thank you for allowing me to chronicle your amazing journey.

— EMILY BERKOWITZ

CONTENTS

Introduction

"God creates; I only assemble..."
GEORGE BALANCHINE

I was perspiring profusely on that impossibly hot, humid day, July 6, 1962, but I would have been just as drenched had it been January in New York. A twenty three year-old Westerner, I was climbing the stairs to the School of American Ballet, about to audition for George Balanchine's New York City Ballet. Not only did I possess the knowledge that Balanchine rarely, if ever, took a dancer from outside his school, but I had been advised repeatedly not to bother to come to New York, as there were no openings in the company for a dancer. Yet I knew I had to come, and try; this had been my greatest dream.

The school was empty and unnaturally silent. How disquieting to enter a place dedicated to the art of movement to music when it was utterly still. The only person I spotted was a secretary. Rather tersely, she told me to change and to go to the back studio. The School, located at that time on Eighty-third Street and Broadway, had all the windows open and large fans operating to combat the heat. Dressed in black tights, a white T-shirt, white socks and white shoes, I warmed up. I was nervous; this tryout could turn our horribly or wonderfully. I was prepared to do the Black Swan male variation taught to me by Alan Howard, one of my teachers in San Francisco. I went into the studio at 2:00 p.m.; at 2:15p.m. George Balanchine walked in.

He was wearing a western-style shirt with the sleeves rolled up. He bowed slightly and shook my hand very graciously. In a soft-spoken, accented voice he asked me what I could do, and I answered him. I had been quite anxious before Mr. Balanchine had entered the studio, but my nervousness evaporated once I shook his hand. I felt comfortable with him immediately. I danced without music, and though I could recognize the sounds of traffic on Broadway, nothing could shake my concentration. When I finished, Mr. Balanchine remarked that I turned just like Lew Christensen used to, and I was quite flattered. Mr. Balanchine then asked me to do *glissade* and *grand jete*, which I did.

We talked. I spoke plainly of myself to Mr. Balanchine: I had been a principal dancer with the San Francisco Ballet; still, I felt I wanted to establish my career in New York. Before leaving

San Francisco, I had a long discussion with Lew Christensen who supported my decision. I was to learn later that he said I was the most reliable dancer he'd ever had. I told Mr. Balanchine that we had been laid off from the San Francisco Ballet for the summer. Mr. B listened and nodded. I told him that I had danced several of his dances in San Francisco, and they had "felt right;" I was so happy when I danced them. More than anything, I genuinely wanted to study with him. Mr. Balanchine, I believe, knew I was sincere. We chatted a bit more, this time, about San Francisco. If I had to summarize that first meeting, I would have to comment that there was immediately a bond of mutual comfort and compatibility. Yet while I knew how famous Mr. Balanchine was, I was to learn how truly great he was.

After we talked a bit, he told me to go change and then see the secretary. I wasn't sure what to think, and when I emerged from the dressing room, it was as before: an empty, too-quiet vast room, just the secretary and me. Mr. Balanchine had gone.

"Go to Capezio for your shoes and City Center for your contract," she said efficiently. Could it be? Balanchine had actually taken me into the New York City Ballet! Despite there being no openings and getting such discouraging warnings from colleagues and friends, Mr. Balanchine had asked me to join the company!

I was exhilarated! Bursting with joy, I traveled to City Center by subway, not even knowing how I got there and not aware of what train I took. My career as a young dancer was launched. Not until my son was born in 1981 was I to have this peak moment again in my life. More recently, I have had it to some extent when I have trained young dancers and watched them grow.

Yet it was not only my life as a dancer that soared that day; I was to forge a close relationship with Mr. Balanchine that was to guide my life for decades, and now, years after his death, still guides my life and helps me make difficult choices. Known always as a brilliant choreographer, one of the greatest in the history of ballet, a musical genius, the co-founder of one of the world's greatest companies, Mr. B was in his own words a teacher first. On his grave are the simple words "ballet master," but his teaching was not limited to dance. Mr. B gave me a life philosophy, a way to live nobly, that has often been overshadowed by his brilliance in the arts. Though this aspect was not well-known, he was deeply spiritual and a genius in more than dance; his comprehension of the significant and the insignificant in life was deep and profound. This brilliantly philosophical, ever-spiritual man was indeed a master teacher to me, but not only in ballet; he taught me how to understand and shape, choreograph, if you will, a meaningful life.

Thus this book tells the story of my life in ballet, especially with Balanchine and the New York City Ballet; of my growth as a dancer, teacher, choreographer, and person; and of the individuals who were my teachers in the art of living, as well as the art of dance. I believe one has strengthened the other. A true master teacher instructs students in much more than just the obvious subject matter. My great teachers — my mother, grandmother, and Mr. Balanchine — endowed me with such gifts. I hope to do at least a bit of the same for my students and readers.

Chapter One: Stars and Signs

"It's the person, who he is, that counts in life..."
STELLA CHILDS HARSAN

Though I have spent much of my life in dance on the East Coast, my roots are truly Western. I grew up in the desert, surrounded by vast space, a peaceful place, awed by the nightly star shows in the desert sky. By day my playground was also the desert, but a brilliantly sunlit one, where my dog and I would run and play games, all the while avoiding the rattlesnakes.

My family fished, built our own home, grew our own vegetables, and even raised our own chickens. Growing up in parts of Arizona, California, Oklahoma and New Mexico, I developed a deep appreciation for the beauty and simplicity of life in the West. These aspects co-mingled with the times in which I grew up the forties and the fifties and have had a lifelong influence on me, as I imagine all of us are influenced by the nature of the times in which we spent our childhoods. For me, the impact of the War years, the fascination of movie musicals, and life in the West influenced me greatly, as did my earliest "master teachers," my grandmother, my mother, and my step-father.

I was born on a January morning in 1939 in Los Angeles, California. It was also the very beginning of World War II. My Swedish father, Eric Severen Ohman, had passed away, so my mother was obligated to work so we could survive. Mom went to work for Lockheed Aircraft, doing soldering, and since she was working during the day, I lived with my grandmother. Grandma and I were very close. She was born Stella Childs, in 1874 in Illinois. When she was ten years old, the family moved to Wichita, Kansas in a covered wagon. They camped against knolls, hiding from Indian tribes. She related that once settled in Kansas, the family had to hide indoors when the Dalton gang and Three-Finger Jack would come into town. Most of the citizens were too scared to go outside, but the outlaws didn't bother anyone; they left them alone.

When Grandma married she became Stella Harsan. Grandma told me family stories. I learned about my grandfather who died before my birth. My grandfather, Franklin Harsan, was a college graduate who was very musically inclined. He studied music and played the piano. My grandfather took my mother, when she was a child, to vaudeville shows. It was their "secret," apparently; Grandpa didn't think my Grandma would approve. On the way home from the vaudeville show, my grandfather would stop off for a game of pool, setting up my mother on the benches. He would end the day by returning home and sitting down at the piano to play all the music he had just heard at the vaudeville show.

My grandmother also told me about my elder sister, Eloyce Paul. It was very disturbing and sad to have had a sister who I never knew; she died at age eighteen, in a car accident, when I was only eleven months old. Grandma was so proud of Eloyce.

My sister, too, had a talent for dance and a budding career. I learned that when Eloyce was quite young she had had pneumonia, and the doctor recommended ballet to help her regain her strength. It was the mid-nineteen-twenties, and the doctor insisted that she attend a solid ballet school that offered proper dance training. He recommended enrolling her in one of only two schools: one of the largest schools west of the Rockies, directed by the Englishman, Ernest Belcher, or a school directed by Theodore Kozlov, a graduate of the Moscow Imperial School and Company. Mr. Belcher's school was picked, and my sister began her study of ballet. My Mom watched my sister in class from a glass-enclosed balcony. Mom was later to use what she picked up to show me some ballet basics at home. In fact, it was in the kitchen, not a ballet studio, and from my Mom, not a ballet teacher, that I learned the five ballet positions.

As I grew up listening to family stories, I am able to share some of the family chronicles. I was told that my sister was a talented dancer. Not only did she study ballet under Ernest Belcher, she was asked to join the Ernest Belcher Dancers. I have an August 28, 1936 program from a performance of this company at the Redlands Bowl in Redlands, California. My sister danced in *Nocturne Moderne,* to music by Thomas Griselle, and *La Gitana* with music by Saint-Saens. Also listed on the program is Marjorie Belcher, Ernest Belcher's daughter. Marjorie grew up with my sister and they went to school together. A wonderful dancer, Marge later married Gower Champion and the pair became very well known as Marge and Gower Champion.

Other dancers among the Ernest Belcher Dancers troupe also became well-known. The program listed Louis Hightower, with whom my sister later toured, as exhibition ballroom dancers. Sadly, he lost his life serving in World War II. Louis' older brother, Bernie, nicknamed Bun, also performed. He combined acrobatics with dance. He was married to my sister Eloyce.

Dancers of this time seemed to cross over the lines between ballroom dancing, ballet, musical performances, and film dancing with ease.

Mr. Belcher's step-daughter was married to Jack Warner's son, and so the involvement of dancers in film was obvious. I was thrilled to learn from my Grandma that the Belcher dancers appeared in the original, silent, Lon Chaney movies. My sister was in *Top Hat* and *Shall We Dance?* She appeared, too, in the film version of the life of Johann Strauss, *The Great Waltz.* I so wish I had known Eloyce.

It was a great blow, a tragedy for all who knew, loved, and were charmed by this exuberant, talented young woman, when she was killed in December of 1939. My Mom explained that before leaving with her husband on the first leg of a tour, Eloyce picked me up out of my crib, and kissed and held me. The accident, I understand, occurred just outside of Montgomery, Alabama, when a lumber truck suddenly barreled down on them. Bernie Hightower saw it coming and was able to leap out of the way, but my sister was unfortunately badly injured. Her chest was crushed and she was rushed to the hospital. My family all traveled to the hospital, where they never left her side. She had sustained very serious injuries. Pneumonia claimed her life a few days later.

In the hospital, as my family waited, prayed, and worried, Bernie entered. His behavior, given the circumstances, was peculiar. Bernie had just minor injuries. When he saw the family, he pulled off his bandages and with an odd smirk, remarked, "See,

I'm fine." His insensitivity to Eloyce's condition was strange; my family did not know what to think.

I was later to learn that Eloyce was planning to leave Bernie after the tour; the marriage was not a happy one. Many years later, Bernie remarried. His second wife was Vera Ellen, who was a star of movies. Vera Ellen Rowe came to visit and chat with my Grandma; we think that perhaps she wanted to learn more about her husband's first wife as well as her husband. Later, Vera Ellen divorced Bernie. It wasn't until many years later that we spotted Bernie dancing with his third wife on *The Ed Sullivan Show*. We learned that he lived off the coast of England. I recall hearing of his passing several years ago.

Grandma was not a morose person who lived in the past. She told me about my sister, father, and grandfather because their spirits were "alive" to her, and became so to me. Moreover, she was very gregarious and had many wonderful, beloved friends who visited us often. I recall Aunt Babe and Aunt Myrtle visiting all the time, all delightful, warm people.

Grandma had a wonderful sense of humor and was forever telling jokes. People were attracted to her and thus our house was filled with friends. I was so often in adult company that I was perhaps more comfortable with them than with children my own age. It was fascinating to listen to their stories, jokes, and Grandma's predictions. My grandmother, you see, had tremendous gifts of perception, what some might call psychic gifts.

I know there are many who are skeptical of this talent (and just as many who pretend to possess psychic abilities) but it does seem to run in my mother's side of the family. Grandma often read cards for her friends. She had prescient dreams, as did my mother, and as I sometimes do. I recall one morning that Grandma said she saw broken glass all over the place in her dream. It unnerved her. A day or two later, she was notified that a friend had been killed in a car accident, and there was shattered glass all over the scene of the tragedy.

Grandma also had some predictions about me. She told me that I would be a dancer, but I would be known for something else, later in life. She also believed that I would spend a great deal of time working with children. Grandma told me that as I got older, I would become more spiritual, philosophical, and more religious. And here I am so many years later, teaching children at my school in Commack, Long Island.

Strange as it may seem, my mother too had prescient dreams. Many years later, when George Balanchine passed away, my mother dreamt of him. She told me that Mr. Balanchine came to her in her dream, saying, "Everyone thinks I am dead but I am not really dead.

I'm only resting." I recall her remarking that it was unusually powerful and real to her.

Perhaps it was Grandma's deep sense of spirituality that was somehow connected with her psychic abilities. Nevertheless, Grandma was a very spiritual person with an abiding faith in God. I was taught by her to love and believe in God. She understood and imparted the intense spiritual nature of existence; she believed that the world we saw around us was only a small part of the universe. Attending church every Sunday was less important than recognizing God and realizing that everyday life had elements of mystery that were part of God's enormous plan, not always apparent to us. She believed that we should have faith and God would be there to guide us.

Grandma also emphasized that it is what is in the human heart, or the kind of person one is, that counts in life. She taught me to recognize and avoid evil. She was ever-conscious of the choices we have to make between good and evil. I guess she knew the temptations of evil were always around, trying to lure us, so one of her favorite expressions was "Get thee behind me, Satan."

Grandma had enormous respect for other religions, too. When the sun would set over a Jewish retirement home across to the west, Grandma would say that the sun was going down over Jerusalem. It became a regular exchange between us. I would ask, "When are we going to have dinner?" My Grandma would reply: "When the sun goes down over Jerusalem." She often told me that Jews were God's chosen people; she had great regard for them.

Our own ancestry was quite mixed. Grandma was English/Welsh/French. My own father had come to the United States from Sweden and met my mother before the War. My father's name in Swedish was Oman, changed to Ohman in the United States. He devoured the newspaper every morning, from front to back, in order to learn English. Grandpa, I was told, had royalty in his lineage. So I guess that makes me Swedish and English and Welsh and French, although it matters very little to me. I've never thought about what nationality anyone was. I believed Grandma's principle that one's character was far more important than any other criteria.

Grandma's spiritual beliefs were largely of a private nature, though she was quite a social person. Although always aware of the spiritual element in life, and guided by it, she was also very much entrenched in day-to-day, practical and fun aspects of life. There was a definite entertainment-world orientation to our lives. Grandma loved movies, especially musicals, and took me to many films. One of my earliest recollections is of being pushed in my stroller in our neighborhood, passing the gas station with the large rotating Flying Horse sign (which I would have to surmise now was a Texaco station), to the old, large Figueroa Movie Theater, not far from my Grandma's house. Much like a movie montage I guess, I was left with certain images from the Figueroa Theater: its huge, dark lobby, hushed environment, soft carpeting throughout, a long concession stand, the smell of the popcorn and sight of the brightly-wrapped candy, and the uniformed ticket taker. The walls were adorned with beautiful posters of coming attractions, commanding my attention. We'd leave the stroller in the lobby and head down the aisle, walking carefully in the dark, save for the small lights on the aisle seats to guide our way, reminiscent of a lit runway. We went to the old Pantages Theater too. It was here that I saw Claude Rains in the musical version of *The Phantom of the Opera*.

Perhaps my grandmother helped turn me into the film buff that I am today. I could add many pages listing all the films I love, such as Basil Rathbone's old *Sherlock Holmes* series. But it is the scary ones that really appeal to me, like the Boris Karloff and Bela Lugosi films. I saw one of my favorite scary films when I was fourteen years old: *The House of Wax* with Vincent Price. I loved him in his films and respected his intelligence and love of art and culture in real life. I would like to have met him. Another scary favorite is the 1945 version of Oscars Wilde's *Portrait of Dorian Gray.*

I always loved the classic silent films of the great Lon Chaney Senior, whose movements I studied as a young dancer, to help my mime for ballet. I was especially a fan of his starring role as the deformed Phantom who haunts the Paris Opera House in the 1925 silent film version of *The Phantom of the Opera.* I had been a fan of Phantom since that visit to the Pantages Theater with my grandmother when I was five years old to see the 1943 version with the great Claude Rains as the Phantom. It also starred Nelson Eddy and Susanna Foster. In fact, the half mask that Claude Rains designed for the Phantom was later used for the 1986 Andrew Lloyd Weber Broadway musical version. A great film!

Maybe I have always been enthralled with movies and musicals because I was born in a period when they were thriving. *Gone with the Wind, Wuthering Heights, Stagecoach* and *The Wizard of Oz* were major films when I was born. I saw all the great ones as a child: *Laura, Portrait of Jenny, The Ghost and Mrs. Muir, All About Eve, Sabrina,* and *The Treasure of the Sierra Madre.* I still love the movies of the 1930s, 1940s, and 1950s. Among my favorites are *An American in Paris, Moulin Rouge,* and *Lust for Life.*

You would think, then, that with all my family's

artistic talents and inclinations, my sister's dance background, and growing up on movie musicals, that I would have had a clear direction early in life toward a career in dance or music. Most, I think, would guess that I started dance classes at a very young age, worked hard, devoted myself completely to my art, and followed a straight path to the dance world. Actually, I quit dance after just one lesson, and I wasn't to resume it again until I was twelve and a half years old, which is considerably older than most begin dance training. My first dance class, in fact, was a disaster. When I was four, my grandmother brought me to Meghlins Dance School. All the famous movie stars Judy Garland, Donald O'Connor, Mickey Rooney studied dance at Meghlins.

I was placed in a class of only girls, and I guess that I was quite a novelty as the solitary boy in the class. As a result, the girls crowded around me, talking and asking me questions. It was a wonderful welcome into the world of dance, but it ended abruptly when the teacher reprimanded me, in front of the whole class, for the girls' unruly behavior. I am happy to say I didn't run crying from the room or hang my head in shame; instead, I told off the teacher! I yelled right back, feeling that she was unfair. With an early flair for theatrical moves, I stormed out of the class and was not to see the inside of a dance class again for the next eight and a half years. It took the great Gene Kelly (in *An American in Paris*) to convince me to give dance another spin.

Though enthralled with the world of entertainment, the reality of a world at war certainly shaped our lives too. When I was between four and five-years old, Grandma had me stand in the doorway when the lights went out and the sirens went on. We had to close our blinds too. These blackout times occurred up and down the West Coast after Pearl Harbor was bombed several years before. We were on alert since there was widespread and serious concern that the coast would be attacked. Grandma had a radio in the front room, and we'd stop everything to listen to FDR's voice. We had to use food stamps to buy meat and other items. Canned Spam was a staple of our diet but coffee was in short supply. Somehow Grandma found time to be involved in sending packages to servicemen overseas.

The ongoing war, the escape and bliss of movies, loads of friends, and lots of love from my Grandma all shaped my early life. Perhaps it was attention to all things spiritual, to the unseen but felt, and the importance of people's natures rather than their wealth or material possessions, that was the lasting gift from my Grandma.

I learned too, to recognize that fighting evil didn't only occur between armies across the seas but between individuals in the everyday world. I learned to recognize goodness and evil from my Grandma, and to make the right choices. As a result, I have cared little for material possessions or personal wealth in life, but I have been richly rewarded by calling friends and colleagues the noble and honorable George Balanchine, Lincoln Kirstein, my students, board members, and so many others. Grandma taught me too that children should be helped and paid attention to; they are special, and they are the future. My Grandma lived well into her eighties, long enough to see me as a successful dancer. It made her happy. I was glad to return the joy she gave and shared with me.

Chapter Two: Dance Sprouts
in Western Soil

"Whatever you do, give it your all"
IRENE OHMAN PHILLIPS

L ife was to change in 1944, when I was five
years old. Traveling by bus to and from
her job at Lockheed Aircraft, my Mom,
Irene Ohman, met a nice man, a Los Angeles
bus driver named Eddie Phillips. Eddie had two
daughters from his first marriage, Margaret and
Beverly. He liked kids, and me, and I guess that
is one of the reasons Mom liked him. When
Eddie became my step-father, I really gained a
father. He was very good to me, a hard worker,
and a good supporter of the family. We loved one
another. So at five years of age, my master teachers
became predominantly my mother and step-father.

Right after the war was over, my Mom and
Eddie were married and Eddie joined the
Southern Pacific Railroad as a fireman. This meant
a great deal of traveling, and so began my love

of the West, and the desert, the spaciousness of which seemed to beget freedom, and the simple beauty of the desert landscape. Since Eddie was always being transferred from one city to another, we took our home with us, living in our trailer in Arizona, Oklahoma, and New Mexico. I came to know and love the desert. Its knolls and cacti became intriguing, then familiar and beautiful sights. Those who aren't familiar with desert knolls would probably be enthralled with their configuration: the sand or land rising at about a thirty degree angle, with a sudden straight drop-off. Some knolls can be as high as a two or three story building. They were often a shade of gray or of red clay. This is the architecture of the desert.

At first, before we had the trailer, we traveled in our 1941 Ford sedan and lived in housing units. They were adequate and all looked alike, resembling army barracks. Each had a number, like A1, A2, A3 and so on. When we traveled by car, I made a bed in the back seat. We crossed the Colorado River many times. Often, when we wanted to bed down at a motel, we found only "no vacancy" signs, so we had to sleep in the car.

On one of our trips we acquired a small Doberman Pinscher. I named her Lady, as she was one. We became inseparable. She slept at the foot of my bed every night. I'd let her out first thing in the morning and she'd race out into the desert. All I had to do was clap, and she'd run back. We would run together, just me and Lady, across the seemingly endless expanse of desert. What a sense of incredible, physical freedom. On one such occasion, I was running and suddenly found I was going to fall into a rattlesnake pit if I didn't leap across it. It was too late to stop, because if I'd stop short, I'd surely tumble into the pit. It was about three feet wide, filled with intertwining, slithering baby rattlers. I held my breath, and leaped after Lady, and felt lucky that we had made it across. I guess leaping was something I learned to do at a young age, out of necessity, not artistic beauty.

Rattlesnakes were a constant danger. Eddie loved to fish and taught me well. Once, on a fishing trip, we had gone up into the mountains, and we were late leaving the camp. The car got stuck in a ditch and it just wouldn't budge, no matter how we struggled and pushed. There wasn't another car or human being in sight. It was growing dark when we realized we would have to camp out in the car for the night. The worst part of being stuck was that we couldn't even exit our vehicle because the rattlesnakes were crawling all around the car. We turned on the car lights to scare the snakes, but that was a temporary exodus only because we had to turn the lights off to preserve the car battery. We stayed put, got through the night, and in the morning, examined the numerous tracks made by the rattlesnakes all around the car. It was unnerving, but we had outwitted them.

Despite its perils, the desert was a source of endless beauty and freedom. The knolls are beautiful as is the prairie. The beauty of the desert isn't only because of the scenery. I found a sense of freedom in the enormous open spaces of the desert. There were no boundaries, nothing to enclose or restrict movement; one could experiment as long as one wanted to. The desert was hot and dry during the day, and cold at night. Although we had serious wind and sand storms, the desert was as beautiful at night as in the day. In the darkness, the desert sky was rich with stars. I watched shooting stars and studied the configuration of clusters of stars. I knew I was a small part of this incredible mystery of the universe.

Since Eddie was always being transferred from one city to another, we only lived for a while in each place. I was happy though; I had Lady, my family, and a fantastic desert playground. My schooling, however, was erratic. I attended kindergarten when I lived in Los Angeles with my grandmother but it wasn't steady until we settled in 1945-46 in San Bernardino.

After several years of traveling between Arizona, New Mexico, Oklahoma and California, Eddie finally quit as a fireman and we settled in California, and headed to the San Bernardino

Valley. So although most of my adult life has been spent in large cities, with little space, my early life was in the wide open spaces. Perhaps I would not have become the same kind of dancer, teacher, or choreographer if I had not gained the enormous sense of freedom and space that came from my early surroundings.

We pulled into the Sunset Court trailer camp in San Bernardino. Ever industrious and ambitious, Eddie immediately became interested in buying a Shell filling station which was for sale. He proposed that we pump gas and have a small store for groceries inside. Mom wasn't wild about the idea but felt it would be beneficial if we could stay in one place, so she agreed. We were in business! We called it Phillips Service. I learned at eight and nine years of age to pump gas and clean windshields.

For my eighth birthday, while still living in our trailer, Eddie bought me a guitar. We couldn't have or afford a piano. Eddie loved Western music or what my Mom referred to as hillbilly music. My hands were too small to go around the frets of the guitar so when we finally settled in San Bernardino, we found a great guitar teacher, Jimmy Saxon, who suggested putting a bar in at the top of the frets to make it a steel guitar or Hawaiian guitar. He gave me a bar and steel finger and thumb pick. Jimmy and I got along so well. He was a wonderful teacher. We would have playing competitions to see who could play the *Steel Guitar Rag* both faster and more correctly. I learned to sight read and memorized almost 200 pieces. I learned to play lots of old folk music, like *Those Endearing Young Charms* and *The Old 97*, among others. I also played Stephen Foster compositions and those of Irving Berlin, including *White Christmas*. I seemed to learn music quickly, which certainly was a great help once I joined the New York City Ballet. I studied steel guitar from the time I was eight until I was twelve and a half, when I changed my mind about studying dance.

After a few years of pumping gas, both Mom and Eddie were ready for a change. Eddie went over to Colton, a small berg near San Bernardino, and applied for a job with Southern Pacific, working as a foreman in the yards. In an interim position, Eddie worked for Mr. Greenberg in his furniture store. Eddie always swore he was the best boss he ever had and hated to part when the position of foreman came through at Southern Pacific.

Eddie and Mom found a new housing development with lots that previously had been pastures for cattle or farms. It was on Del Rosa Avenue, and they decided to buy a 50 by 150 foot lot. We parked the trailer on our lot and Eddie started us right away on constructing a driveway. Eddie of course wanted to build a house. We lived in the trailer while he started the foundation for the house. Eddie brought home old unwanted railroad box car flats to construct most of the walls. This was a brilliant idea, I thought; it didn't cost a cent. He bought the two by fours and everything else. We helped Eddie dig the cesspool, twenty feet deep, and we walled it up with brick. I helped put in ditches for water pipes. Eddie built a large addition to the front, and put in hardwood floors. Once the house was finished, we built a two-car garage, and planted a huge front lawn with roses along the driveway, true to our street name Del Rosa I guess. I did a lot of shoveling then, and even later, and I guess it gave me a strong back to lift ballerinas.

It was a great feeling of pride and accomplishment to have helped build our own house. We soon started to raise our own chickens, and grow our own vegetables and fruits. We also had turkeys, and rabbits, all of which I named. We lived off the land completely, and it was a very healthy lifestyle. On the west side of our lot was Patton State Hospital and all around the area were either fields of cattle or orange groves. I walked through the cattle fields every day to get to my elementary school, Warm Springs Elementary School, and was chased by a bull nearly every morning (good training for Balanchine's fast footwork.) On the way home from school, we could snatch a few oranges right off the trees, which only now do I confess to doing.

It was nice in the valley; in the winter I could see the beautiful San Bernardino Mountains capped with snow. We weren't too far for a trip to Big Bear and Lake Arrowhead either. Eddie was a hard worker and liked to have a drink now and again, but never to excess. He made his own beer in our garage and in the summer when it got very hot, some of the beer bottles would explode. He wasn't one to go out drinking, though, or frequent bars. We were self-sufficient, I believe, and everything we had and how we lived were the result of our own labors. I guess we were living the American dream, where with hard work and integrity, anything is possible.

I felt loved by my mother and step-father, and continued playing my guitar. I recall playing for my classmates at school and even at home for close friends and neighbors. When I was about ten years old and living in the trailer while Eddie was building the house, several boys were sitting on the fence watching us. I said "hello." One boy asked another, named Kenny, "Do ya think ya can beat him up?" Kenny answered, "I don't know." I suppose wherever one is San Bernardino, New York, everywhere young people need to prove themselves. Kenny McDonald and I got along well enough somehow. Though he was a tough kid, we used to play ball sometimes. At the age of fifteen, though, he got a girl pregnant, and I never learned what became of him thereafter.

My childhood was a normal one. My mother taught me early the kind of discipline and motivation that goes along with success in any career. I went to bed by 9:00 p.m. I liked to sleep late on Saturday mornings and listen, in bed, to the birds chirp outside and hear my stepfather working outside on his latest project, as well as hear the sound of the chickens and turkeys and ducks. I got good grades at school, and continued to play the guitar there, especially at school functions, but I never danced. I was a bit shy in the girl department until I was older; I imagine that makes me a late bloomer. I did have secret crushes on girls. I fell for eleven-year old Paula when I was thirteen, and was mad about her.

I suppose the only female with whom I was openly affectionate in those young years was Lady, my Doberman. By now she was older, and we got another dog, Mike. Later it was Mazie, a Cocker Spaniel I would grow to love so. We never had cats, and yet years later after moving to Long Island, I had only feline pets. They seem to be more patient with us busy humans than dogs are.

As before, movies, especially musicals, were a major part of our leisure time. There were no Schubert Theaters in San Bernardino, and I guess I was not very knowledgeable, as a young man, about the arts, but we did have M.G.M. movies.

The landmark event igniting my interest in dance was seeing Gene Kelly in *An American in Paris*. When I was twelve, my parents took me to see this treasure. I was transformed. I knew that was what I wanted to be: a dancer like Gene Kelly. He became my idol. After seeing Gene Kelley's incredible dancing on the screen, I told my Mom that I wanted to be a dancer like him. I still had never seen a ballet.

I guess some parents would have shrugged off a child's comments or tried to dissuade their son from a career in the arts. Fortunately, Mom was very accepting; I never had to defend my choice or explain it to her. In fact, it was simply understood between us. She had a great feeling for the arts too, and understood my passion. Her philosophy was that if that was what I wanted to do, then my priorities should be getting the proper training and giving it my full energy and dedication. This was the beginning of her full-fledged support and encouragement. One of her principles about which she reminded me often was to develop my God-given talents to their ultimate potential. This was a must, in her eyes. She also believed that every person must use his gifts for the betterment of humankind. So her reaction to my request to take tap lessons *a la* Gene Kelly was to take me very seriously. How fortunate for me!

Her advice was to get solid, classical ballet training instead of only tap lessons. She told me that with ballet training, I could do any type of dance. How she knew this, I am not sure, but she was absolutely right about getting a solid classical training. I find too many parents today do not realize the difference between good classical ballet training and what I call "fast food" dancing schools. The latter are abundant but generally don't teach the right techniques or give children the right foundation; they often just "train" them for a year-end show for parents and relatives. Instead of working all year on ballet basics and the proper techniques, they are taught only to perform a specific sequence of steps for a specific number for a show.

So at the age of twelve and a half with no dance training at all, we began to investigate ballet schools and teachers. Though we hadn't seen Mr. Belcher for years, we contacted him again. This lovely man, now in his late seventies, could still kick his leg up to his shoulder. My ballet training with Mr. Belcher, Vera Lynn, and Charles Baker, wonderful teachers all, began in earnest.

Mom also introduced me to the ballet as an audience member. When I was twelve and a half, America Ballet Theater, known then as Ballet Theater, came to the San Bernardino Theater and Mom took me to see a performance. It was my first ballet. This special event was preceded by articles in the newspaper about Igor Youskevitch's great leaps. He was the premier *danseur* and had been an athlete too. The virile Johnny Kriza convinced me that ballet for men wasn't all swans and guys in tights. The ballet stars with Ballet Theater were amazing! We saw Johnny Kriza in *Billy the Kid*, and the great Alicia Alonzo, Nana Gollner, and Igor Youskevitch in the *Black Swan pas de deux*. I also saw Jerome Robbins' *Fancy Free*. The dancers, the music, and the steps swirled delightfully in my mind long after the performance was over. I was even able to envision it, night after night, as I lay in my bed. It left a lifelong impression.

Eddie though, didn't quite understand the ballet. His opinion was that it was an aristocratic snobbish art and only for the rich. But we shared other types of hobbies and interests. Eddie always followed boxing, and we followed a match when fights were broadcast on the radio. When I was about ten years old, I recall seeing a great fight film called *The Set Up*, a film about an unfair system that I think was tremendously underrated.

Still, I was further intoxicated with dance after seeing films like *Singing in the Rain*, with Gene Kelly, and later, *Seven Brides for Seven Brothers*. In fact, I became enthralled with movie musicals. Once, my parents became very irritated and angry with me for coming home late, hours after I was expected, because I had stayed at the movies to watch *Carousel* for a second time. Into the kitchen I walked, gushing with admiration and awe for Jacques d'Amboise. Who could have predicted this non-dancing young teen would later have the thrill of dancing with one of his idols, Jacques d'Amboise?

D'Amboise is and was an incredibly talented dancer and partner. He was one of the greatest instinctive dancers I have ever known. He became a very good friend too, once I joined the New York City Ballet. I have wonderful memories of our going camping in upstate New York together. Later I was to also admire and know Eddie Villella, one of the most graceful dancers and highest jumpers I have ever seen.

While my mother never danced herself, she had an intuitive sense of what was necessary, such as hard work, dedication, and discipline. She set a daily routine, which on a school day would include returning from school, having a piece of one of her homemade cakes, and then immediately practicing my instrument. Play could follow until dinner, and then it was homework time.

She set an example as a hard worker too. I remember hearing about one of her first jobs, working for the telephone company as a switchboard operator. She learned quickly and worked hard, but decided not to continue because another employee was constantly irritating her. Her absence from work didn't go unnoticed though. Her boss called her, and asked why she had been absent. Mom told the boss that another woman was bothering her. His response was "Irene, you do the work of three people. Come back." She did, and the other woman never troubled her again.

I loved ballet classes. Perhaps some of its initial appeal was the classical music, which I had adored from an early age. By the time I began ballet training, I not only loved classical music but understood it as well. I liked the popular music of Bill Haley and the Comets but I adored classical music and opera. When I entered my teen years, Eddie claimed that I would eat them out of house and home (a common complaint of parents of teens, I think). He also couldn't fathom how I could listen to classical music. I started sneaking classical records from the library into the house but he'd catch me and ask my Mom, "Why does Frank always sneak those classical records in his back window?" I was in love with the theme from *Swan Lake* so I played it over again and again, driving Eddie nuts. Whenever he heard the beginning of *Swan Lake*, he'd say to Mom, "There goes that kid playing that moaning music again."

I was fortunate to have my Mom's full support for my artistic drives. I suppose my Mom believed that people are born with certain inclinations and so she fully understood and encouraged my artistic propensities. It does make me wonder about destiny and whether we are all given certain drives that we must follow.

My Mom, just like her mother, my grandmother, was also endowed with a spiritual nature and psychic talents. My mother thoroughly believed in reincarnation. She believed that in a former life she was a Castilian Spanish dancer, which might account for her fondness for dance and other artistic forms. She was a very outgoing, intelligent, and funny woman who could assess a person's character in a minute, and was seldom wrong. She told me often: "You've got to know people better, quicker," her way of saying that I was perhaps too trusting and easy-going. She read many books on psychic and spiritual subjects, like Edgar Cayce's books.

Like her own mother, my Mom saw the world through a spiritual lens. She believed that when a person passed on, their deceased loved ones were waiting to greet and welcome him. It was a feast rather than a sad and depressing occurrence. We would have many talks about spiritual themes. She once told me that there was no such thing as time. Time, she explained, was invented by man. In eternity, there is no time. The body is temporary, she believed, while the spirit is forever. Her ideas dovetailed with Mr. Balanchine's, and later they could talk on the same level and with mutual understanding. Mr. B would say that this was not the real world; the real world was the spiritual world. "This is shadow world," I remember Mr. Balanchine saying. My Mom believed the same.

While my Grandma had cards, my Mom had astrological charts. In fact, after Suzanne Farrell left the New York City Ballet in 1969, Mr. Balanchine asked about my mother's knowledge of astrology and he asked if she could do his astrological chart. After acquiring some necessary facts, like his birth date and year, my Mom studied his chart. Though unfamiliar with his personal life, her assessment was, "Someone has left you whom you care deeply about, but don't worry; she's going to return." How right she was.

Years later, when I was a member of the New York City Ballet, she grew very fond of Mr. Balanchine and they became friends. When she was living in New York, and I was dancing with the City Ballet, she'd meet Mr. B in the street and they'd chat often about their similar spiritual outlook. She often felt she was going to bump into him. Their chats would never be about me; I was rarely mentioned. Mom never asked Mr. B for anything for me; she wanted no favors. They had their own bond. She understood and appreciated his genius. They both were very perceptive when it came to human nature and both were very spiritual. Mr. B hated gossip and he too was an expert in detecting insincerity.

Mom also believed, and instilled in me, that loyalty accompanies love. Thus she was a very loyal friend and admirer of Mr. Balanchine. When the critics bashed Balanchine's *PAMTGG (Pan Am Makes the Going Great)*, a minor work, and accused him of no longer being able to create great works, my Mom and I felt the critics were crazy; we never doubted his genius. When the Stravinsky Festival opened shortly thereafter to rave reviews, many critics suddenly changed their positions, calling him a genius once more. On another occasion, my Mom was waiting for me at the stage door, and saw Mr. B leaving with a young woman on his arm. She heard gossipers starting to comment about what was a benign occurrence, and Mom chastised them, defending Mr. B. In fact, Mom and I often talked about Mr. B as if he were part of the family. When I joined the New York City Ballet, and would occasionally receive offers from Ballet Theater or other companies to be a principal dancer, my Mom told me that it was better to be in the corps of George Balanchine's New York City Ballet than a principal dancer with another company.

Chapter Three: The Grand Jete of Faith

"There's no stopping and no detours on the road to your career. Just go straight down the road to your goal."
IRENE OHMAN PHILLIPS

Dance was becoming a bigger part of my life as I turned thirteen and fourteen years-old. I was studying ballet with Charles Baker and I had to take class with little girls. There I was, the only boy of course, wearing tights. Now, so many years later, I have just one boy in my school. Some aspects of the ballet world haven't changed, I guess.

By the age of fourteen, I had also gotten pretty good at tap dancing. My family and I were avid fans of the television talent show, *Hollywood Opportunities*, broadcast on station KTLA. One week, after watching the program, Mom asked me, "Do you want to do it?" Her tone and expression revealed her understanding of how difficult it was to enter the world of Hollywood, but it also conveyed a sense of exciting possibilities. "Here you are," she said, assessing me, "a corn fed kid from San Bernardino, trying to break into the world of entertainment." As she and Eddie had realized many of their dreams a home of their own, a business, and a healthy lifestyle, so she encouraged me to pursue mine. There was never a time when she advised me to abandon my goals, even though this country kid had no connections, no major or famous patron, no financial backing, and was geographically so removed from the sophisticated world of New York ballet. Yet we lived in a time when all things seemed possible, as long as one worked hard and had integrity. So, when my Mom suggested being a contestant on *Hollywood Opportunities*, I thought, "Why not?" It sure seemed possible.

Mom called the station and arranged for an audition. My step-father, my Mom, and I were on our way to Los Angeles a few weeks later. The audition was held right on the stage of the television studio, and there were quite a few teenagers there, around my age and older. There were budding pianists; male and female singers (all vocalizing); near-perfect jugglers; nervously harmonizing duos; horn players; and the like.

I was surprised at the size of the television studio itself; it was immense! Our television screen was small, though encased in a large solid wood box, making everything appear rather close and cozy. Wearing my tuxedo, I warmed up in the lobby, and then sat in the audience with the other youthful contenders. I was nervous as I waited for my turn, but a curious reversal occurred. As soon as I was on stage, my anxiety abated and I was comfortable and enjoyed myself. It was the first time I had experienced real live performing, and I reveled in it. Perhaps I was a real ham, but it is a pattern I have continued all my life. I am actually grateful for it. Once a professional dancer, I found that I was a stage dancer, not a rehearsal or class dancer. I always worked hard in class and rehearsals, but I came alive and gave my all during the performance.

The host of *Hollywood Opportunities* was actor Richard Arlen, a film star popular in the late 1930s and 1940s. He was sitting in the audience during the auditions. And to my delight, I was actually picked! A few weeks later, I was back for the live show. There were about eight to ten contestants now. Nervous beforehand, I forced myself to concentrate on what I was going to do. When my turn came, Mr. Arlen interviewed me and then I danced to Cole Porter's *It was Just One of Those Things*, wearing a top hat and tails. The show was broadcast live. When all the contestants had finished, we all lined up and they used an applause meter to determine the winners. I was shocked, but I had actually tied for first place with a female singer! When I was given a wrist watch as a prize, I immediately said, "Thanks, but this is for her" and offered it to the co-winner. It seemed like the gentlemanly thing to do.

Though thrilled, I couldn't publicly enjoy being a winner. In those days, as a male who wanted to be a dancer, I knew I'd be given a hard time by other students. So I had to keep my triumph quiet. There will come a time, I believed, when I'd really get somewhere and then my peers would know about it.

I enjoyed Highland Junior High School, but truly my academic classes were taking a back seat to my interest in dance. I had a racer bike that I lived on, and school friends, and I was comfortable in our Del Rosa Avenue home with our flourishing garden, but I began to yearn for New York and a career. My life was filled with suburban pleasures, but I had ideas and dreams of glamorous New York and theater. I was still enthralled with films, especially MGM musicals, and they only increased my interest in dance.

My dreams about a dancing career were based on a patchwork comprised of snippets of information I read, threads of glamorous dance sequences from movie musicals, the very occasional ballet companies on tour in the West, and my imagination. I knew Joe DiMaggio married Marilyn Monroe, but I knew very little about the New York City Ballet. I had read in an article when I was thirteen years-old that Maria Tallchief and George Balanchine were married and were major successes in New York but that was the extent and depth of my knowledge.

Occasionally, a ballet company would perform on the West Coast and we would attend. I recall the soloists from the Royal Danish Ballet coming to the Hollywood Bowl in 1957, when Stanley Williams was a member. I didn't get to go to the School of American Ballet or other specialized schools for the performing arts; at thirteen, I didn't know they existed. Yet I knew and I could feel this world was my destiny and my goal, though it was such a blurry vision.

I began to scour the library not just for classical records to sneak into my room, aggravating my classical music foe step-father, but for books on famous dance figures. I read about the period of the Ballets Russes de Monte Carlo, its charter member, Russian-born David Lichine, and his wife, Tatiana Riabouchinska, who, as a "baby ballerina," made her debut at age fifteen. I started to devour volumes on the lives of dancers, including the diary of the famed dancer Nijinsky.

In the fall of 1954, after graduating from Highland Junior High, we moved closer to Los Angeles, settling in Ontario, California. My parents felt being closer to Los Angeles was important because it offered serious dance training. Ontario, near Pomona, was a wonderful suburban area. Euclid Avenue, bordered by trees, ran right down the middle of the town. Up from the main part of the town was Chaffey High School where I spent grades ten, eleven, and twelve. Our one-story house had a big backyard where I liked to pitch horseshoes. My new bedroom was unheated, because of its location in an un-insulated part of the house, but I liked it cold at night, so it was fine. I had a *barre* in the garage to practice right alongside the beer crocks Eddie set up to make his own brew.

I was beginning to formulate my future plans, so while I enjoyed high school, I was focusing beyond those years to a career in dance. My parents and I felt that it would be best if I went into Los Angeles on weekends to study dance with Mr. Belcher, who provided the finest training in our region. I could stay with my grandmother over the weekend. It was exciting; we were laying the foundation for the bridge to my professional dance career.

I felt quite mature and independent in my high school years. Whereas previously Mom had sold Avon cosmetics to pay for my dance lessons, I now did janitorial work for two hours each day after school to pay for my classes with Mr. Belcher, which were twenty-five dollars per lesson, plus my transportation to Los Angeles. I actually earned the money for my dance classes from the age of sixteen onward and I was quite proud about doing so. When the weekend came, I hopped on the bus, and then took a streetcar to Grandma's. I enjoyed this taste of independence.

I began studying with Mr. Belcher, who at the time was in his eighties but was still incredibly limber and agile. An Englishman, he taught me the English style of ballet. It was this same Mr. Belcher, the other Mr. B in my life, who taught me how to pirouette or turn. His dancers were known as the best turners, and even today I teach my students the way Mr. Belcher taught me. "Turn like a coin spinning," he'd say, so I'd stay perfectly upright.

Mr. Belcher treated me as if he was a kind uncle. We were quite close, and we'd spend time chatting as he'd prepare a grilled cheese sandwich and English tea for me. His daughter Marge and her husband Gower Champion were often traveling and working, so Mr. Belcher and I would go to their home in the Hollywood Hills for a swim while they were away.

I certainly wasn't his only student in those days. There was an adorable dark-haired little girl, about five or six, who took lessons from him too. I'd sometimes show her steps or give her brotherly advice. Her name was Angela Cartwright, and she became a successful television actress, appearing in programs like *Lost in Space*.

I studied with Miss Rozelle Frey too. I'd

go to Miss Frey's studio for class, which she taught according to the Cecchetti school of dance. What distinguishes this type of dance are the positions of the arms. While the basic positions are fundamentally the same, the arm movements—the *ports de bras*—are different.

The *adagios* are different too; they are slow and controlled, with lots of bending.

FRANK OHMAN AT MARGE AND GOWER
CHAMPION'S POOL - 1958

Miss Frey had a large studio with high ceilings and wood floors. We had to use a watering can, not rosin, on the floors. There was a makeshift curtain that separated the boys and the girls dressing areas. I got used to that degree of informality and it never troubled me that we didn't have privacy. Most people in the theater don't think much about it. I guess dancers are so physically aware of their bodies that there is usually little self-consciousness about being undressed.

One memorable time, Miss Frey had Mia Slavenska, a friend of hers, teach a master class at the studio. Mia Slavenska was a Yugoslav-born ballerina, choreographer, and teacher with her own company for a time. In the early 1950s she had teamed up with Frederic Franklin, touring with an ensemble group. Miss Slavenska amazed me. I had never seen anyone do a full *adagio* on full *releve* without coming down. Miss Slavenska did it, and I was amazed because she wore flat ballet slippers, not *pointe* shoes. What beautiful challenges were ahead in ballet!

A most fortunate opportunity occurred when I was in eleventh grade. Mr. Belcher talked to a friend who permitted me to take class with Ballet Theater, now known as American Ballet Theater, when they were touring the West. I had idolized Youskevitch as the elegant, premier *danseur* noble. Now I had the joy of seeing Erik Bruhn dancing in *Paquita Pas de Deux*. It was breathtaking. Oh, the perfection of his technique, the elegant, beautiful feet, and turnout! He was about twenty-seven then, reaching his full height as an artist. I had finally seen the idea of clean, beautiful technique fully executed. As a budding dancer, I made this technique a goal of mine; as a fan, I set about trying to get photos of Erik Bruhn.

Back at high school, I rode my bike all over, played a bit of basketball, went to the library, but didn't really get deeply involved in the school. My heart and head were in dance. I could have gone to Chaffey Junior College but this was not my dream. So I was an atypical teenager in this way, but quite typical in other ways.

Like my contemporaries, I was a fan of James Dean and was crushed when he died in the mid-fifties. I was one of so many teens who had identified with him; he had represented all of us misunderstood and confused adolescents. Elvis and rock and roll music were catching on everywhere, and Marlon Brando was the genius actor.

I was very shy with girls in high school. But I recall having a huge crush on the beautiful, gregarious, dark-haired Janet Delozier who lived down the street from me in Ontario. I never got up the nerve to ask her for a date but I had fantasies about her. I was a late bloomer in that area, I suppose. Even when I was older, I had relationships and I was sincere, but still shy.

Despite my interest in dance, I was not ostracized terribly; I really never let the other kids' comments get to me. I kept to myself mostly and took care not to broadcast my rather unusual career interests. I did get a break, socially speaking, in eleventh grade, when I choreographed my first piece and danced to Gershwin's *I Got Rhythm*

which I performed with a girl in my grade, for the
high school show, Chaffey High's Extravaganza.
It brought down the house! From then on,
everyone at school treated me with great respect.
I'd walk through the hall or go to the cafeteria
and kids would congratulate me. Having seen
me in the show, my art teacher, who did tease
me a bit about dancing, seriously announced
to the class that "Frank is going to make it. We
all tease him, but he's the one who is going
to put this town and this school on the map."

Part of my plan to become a dancer was to
graduate early. By taking summer courses, I
was able to graduate midterm, in January, 1957,
just after my eighteenth birthday. And it wasn't
even a week later that I was on the bus to Los
Angeles, to find a job to support myself while I
studied dance. On my bus ride, I thought about
my father who I had never known, and how he
had come to this country with his brothers and
sisters from Sweden. So many hopes and dreams,
some realized, some dashed. My mother used to
speak of Winston Churchill and how much she
admired him as a great man who had helped save
the world from tyranny. What would I achieve
in my life? I felt on the brink of really beginning
my life. Perhaps this was a second birthday.

About four days after I arrived in Los Angeles,
I found a job with the Land Title Insurance

Company. I was to do filing in the map department. I got an apartment near my new employer. The famous Brown Derby was there on Wilshire Boulevard. Mr. Belcher lived nearby and Miss Frey's studio was close, on Alexandria Street. I brought a duffel bag to work with me at Land Title twice a week. When anyone asked me what was in the bag, as people surely did, I told them it was my bowling bag. I convinced people that I was an avid bowler. Actually, it was my ballet bag, but I didn't want any odd looks or rumors. On Friday nights, after class, I liked to go to the movies. It was a thrill to be eighteen years old, studying ballet, working, and living in my own apartment in Los Angeles.

It was around this time that Igor Youskevitch and Alicia Alonso, world-class dancers, were holding auditions for a two-week engagement of *Giselle* at the Greek Theater at Griffith Park in Los Angeles. I did get an audition with Igor, and it was he who advised me to go to New York. I grew very excited, my thoughts focusing on the East Coast. Not surprisingly, within a few months, I was fired from Land Title Insurance. My mind was so consumed with dance and I had just auditioned for Igor Youskevitch, so that it is no wonder that I was fired for "lack of interest." My work was fine, they said, I just didn't seem all that interested. Right they were.

But it was the only time in my life that I was fired.

So, since I did not have a job at that time anyway, my Mom and I decided to finally go to New York, where I could study at the School of American Ballet for two weeks. We hoped too to see if it was financially viable for me to stay in New York and pursue my career.

We took the train from California to New York, which took us about three days and three nights. New York was astounding: big, fast, and serious. The sight of the skyscrapers was amazing, since even Los Angeles didn't have tall buildings at the time. Everything moved so quickly, including the subways, the underground train system. It was, as others have said, overwhelming. Mom and I got a room at a hotel on Fifty-fourth Street and Broadway, near Times Square. I took classes at the School of American Ballet and with the New York City Ballet company at City Center. Mom and I went to the old Metropolitan Opera House, then on Forty-third Street near Times Square, to see Ballet Theater. We sat in the fourth ring of the balcony, quite a height, but it didn't matter to me. I saw Erik Bruhn, a masterful dancer with a gorgeous classical technique. The performance was entrancing.

The School of American Ballet, founded by George Balanchine and Lincoln Kirstein, was on Eighty-third Street and Broadway at that time.

Anatole Oboukhoff and Pierre Vladimiroff, both leading dancers of Russian's famed Mariinsky Theater and graduates of the Imperial School of Ballet, were teaching the boy's classes. I had the pleasure of meeting Francisco Moncion and Nicholas Magallanes, both in the class, both future New York City Ballet dancers. The students and the teachers were all sincerely helpful.

My mother and I decided to go over to City Center, where the company rehearsed, and where I met Janet Reed. Janet had danced with Ballet Theater in the 1940s, and then with the City Ballet in the 1950s. She became Ballet Mistress at the New York City Ballet. Janet was so nice to me and gave me sound advice. One of her first nuggets of wisdom was to never leave one job before you have another. I was a bit naive too when it came to my appearance. My hair was very long, so I wore a hairnet in classes. I think I indulged too much in my bottle of pine cologne. Janet advised me about this too.

Since our modest resources were rapidly being depleted and I gathered that I would need to get work if I were to study in New York, I headed to the unemployment office near Christopher Street to see if I could land a stock room or mail room job. Nothing seemed promising. I once again turned to my caring teachers, my mother and Mr. Belcher, who advised me to return to California, and work towards dancing with the Christensens in San Francisco before trying to get into a New York company. I was disappointed. I had sipped my first real taste of the intoxicating world of New York dance. But Mr. Belcher echoed the words of my mother, and advised me to get some further training and experience in San Francisco with the Christensens.

As a nineteen-year old, briefly breathing in this dance world, glimpsing the classes, the company, the stages, the people whom I had seen on stage or read about, I felt great pangs of desire to stay, to join them, to dance. Not yet, my mother patiently advised. At the time it seemed like primarily a financial barrier. I realize now that it was also my need to grow both technically and professionally.

So we returned to the West Coast. I worked in the summer of 1957 with David Lichine, a friend of Miss Frey's, in his Beverly Hills school. I've been blessed to work with such talent and genius throughout my career, an apt description for Mr. Lichine. A dancer and choreographer, David joined Colonel De Basil's Ballets Russes de Monte Carlo, where he created so many roles, including one of the two leading males in *Cotillon*. He had choreographed wonderful pieces for Ballet Theater, especially in the late 1930s and 1940s, including *Helen of Troy* to music by Offenbach, and *Graduation Ball*. He was a very fine choreographer.

In 1957, he was choreographing and staging ballets for upcoming performances at the Santa Monica Bowl. I was to dance in *Graduation Ball* and a new piece set to Dvorak's *New World Symphony*. Mr. Lichine's wife, Tatiana Riabouckinska, had been a "baby ballerina" with Balanchine in Europe. So, I took the bus out to Mr. Lichine's studio on weekends. He was the first famous choreographer I ever worked with, and what a grand experience. Was he ever fun! Utterly unpretentious,

Mr. Lichine was quite funny. He wouldn't sit in a chair during rehearsals, but on the floor, in front of the dancers. He was the only choreographer I ever worked with who did that. He referred to me as "the young one." In the *Graduation* ballet, he played the headmistress; he had to dress up in drag and he was hysterical. He was a truly multi-talented man.

I had gotten a taste of the electric and growing world of New York ballet, and I had devoured all that the Los Angeles area had to offer. A middle-sized meal awaited me in San Francisco. I had to get further training and become part of a professional dance company. No detours, my mother had said. So I made my grand *jete,* with great faith and hope, leaping into San Francisco's dance world.

Chapter Four: Dancing and Dishing

"I don't want people who want to dance;
I want people who have to dance."
GEORGE BALANCHINE

My leap of faith took me from home to San Francisco, where my mother and Mr. Belcher had advised me to study with the internationally-known and respected Christensens. Dancers of uncommon strength and technique, both Lew and his brother Harold had danced with Lincoln Kirstein and George Balanchine's company, Ballet Caravan which preceded the New York City Ballet.

The Christensens's roots were in vaudeville, and besides ballet, they had danced in musicals as well. After serving in the army in World War II, Lew returned to dance with Mr. B's Ballet Society. Always possessing a larger vision and perspective as well as sharp detailed insights, like simultaneously having telescopic and microscopic vision, Mr. B advised Lew

Christensen to focus on San Francisco. A third brother, William Christensen, was a professor in theater ballet at the University of Utah, where he established ballet and choreography courses offered along with academic subjects. I never imagined that they would have me learning the Balanchine repertoire, the very dances I was to do when I joined the New York City Ballet.

When I arrived in San Francisco in the fall of 1958 I went to their school at Sixteenth Street and Alexandria. Harold Christensen was in the office. A tall, slender man with greying hair, Harold was very polite and formal. I told him my name and my dance background, explaining that I had studied with Mr. Belcher, Ms. Frey, and Mr. Lichine. He showed me around the school, and watched me dance. He told me to come back for Lew's men's class that evening. I told him I was looking for a job, and he immediately gave me a half scholarship, and a part-time job, cleaning windows, putting in light bulbs, and doing other odd jobs at a smaller dance school run by Gisella Caccialanza, Lew's wife, and Ruby Asquith, Harold's wife. Both were ballerinas of note; they had danced with Ballet Caravan too.

I still needed a larger income to get an apartment and survive in San Francisco, so I took the advice of my mother and headed to the Southern Pacific Hospital for work. Mom suggested I work in the

Hospital's kitchen, because, she said, "you'll always be guaranteed that you will eat." As usual, her advice was sound and I got a job in the hospital kitchen. Just across the street, I found a room for sixteen dollars a month. The bath was down the hall, under the stairs. My living quarters were now much smaller than my previous Los Angeles apartment, but the City of San Francisco easily kept me from spending much time in my room, and enabled me to conserve some money too.

I loved my classes. Harold Christensen was the technique teacher; I learned so many basics from him. A meticulous techniques instructor, Harold stressed the proper alignment or correct standing position, as well as the need to be centered and to maintain proper turnout. The West was surely lucky for so long to have had him and his school.

Lew, on the other hand, conveyed the power of the male dancer. His classes were very exact too, and he had an uncanny ability to know what each of us needed to work on. It took me a bit of time to become accustomed to his classes. They were more physical and more exacting. The results, though, were the development of specific skills and a cleaner technique. Lew told me that if I worked hard, he could foresee taking me into the company. I was prepared to do just that. A very musical person, Lew played his cello in his back room office, located deliberately, I believe, behind the wardrobe department and far away from the zestfully ambitious, advice-giving parents, critics all, and away from rambunctious students, energetic visiting siblings, and so forth. All my subsequent strength with the New York City Ballet, I believe, had its early roots in my training with the Christensens.

But when I wasn't working or taking classes, I was falling in love. No, I still was shy around women and still hadn't had an affair, though I would have liked to, but I thought it might distract me from my professional goal. No, it was San Francisco itself that was winning my heart. I loved living in San Francisco with its fog that is unlike the fog in any other location. What a romantic city! I've still not heard anything like its fog horns at night. I loved Market Street and the cable cars. I enjoyed Aliotos at Fisherman's Wharf and the Spaghetti Factory in what was then the beatnik area. The Wharf area also offered Seal Island huge rocks out in the water which drew seals to it, for sunbathing or frolicking and I found their antics irresistible. Now I think of similarities between San Francisco and Europe, like the cobblestone streets. The bay was so beautiful. Later, I went to the Golden Gate Park and the Japanese Tea Gardens on Sundays and fed the squirrels.

On my day off, I went to the movies along Market Street. I could go in at 11:00 a.m. and emerge at 6:00 p.m., having seen six cartoons and three feature films. That is my definition of a great day! I remember seeing *The Apartment* with Jack Lemmon, and, at the Alexandria Theater, near the school, seeing *South Pacific*.

I was just twenty, and I didn't know many people my age or with my interests in this new city, so at times when I was lonely I would take the cable car to the Wharf, or Chinatown. Once I was a bit shaken up by an overly friendly orderly I had met at my job at the hospital. We talked from time to time of music, movies, and so on, and he invited me to have lunch at his apartment. That was just one of the homosexual advances I have rebuffed in my life. While it has never been my nature, many colleagues and friends over the years have been gay. My philosophy has always been to live your life the way you want, as long as you don't hurt someone.

I had a number of jobs while in San Francisco. Besides working in the hospital kitchen, I also worked as an elevator operator there, and while it was not very interesting or challenging, I did enjoy talking with the patients. Sometimes, I had as many as four different jobs at a time; sometimes, there were gaps between jobs that were trying. I remember once I had no money at all. Perusing a market one day, I found thirty dollars in the shop and reported it. As no one came forward to claim the cash, I got to keep it. Talk about gifts from heaven! That was half a month's rent for me.

Good to his word, Lew asked me to join the company in the summer of 1959. I was now a member of the San Francisco Ballet! It seemed like I had worked forever toward this goal, though it had only been two years since I had graduated from high school. I had to join the American Guild of Musical Artists known as AGMA immediately, and learn parts for the upcoming performance, my first, at the Red Rocks Amphitheater outside of Denver, Colorado.

Some find that the realization of long-awaited dreams can be disappointing; mine was not, but it was mixed with unanticipated sadness. My mother was visiting me in San Francisco when I joined the company, and during her visit, my step-father Eddie had a fatal accident at home. He had fallen, and suffered a head injury. Poor Eddie! I had known him as my dad since I was a little boy. When I was young, he was my pal. When I was in my teens, I was a bit of a smart-aleck, and though I had grown out of it, I felt a bit guilty about giving him a difficult time. I feel though that he always understood what was in my heart. I was so sorrowful that Eddie never saw me in a professional ballet. He was just fifty-two years old when his life ended.

My Mom had to take care of the details following Eddie's death and I had to return to

San Francisco to prepare for Red Rocks, my first professional performance with the San Francisco Ballet. I was beginning to see one aspect of being a professional: one must continue with one's work despite personal issues and losses. Do we ask too much of ourselves when we do that? Does this attitude make us more admirable or less human? I don't quite have the answers. I do know that I felt the blow of Eddie's death.

I was rescued to some degree by the exquisite setting for my first performance with the San Francisco Ballet. Performing in the awesome Red Rocks Amphitheater was also meaningful to me as I remembered my stepfather, the person who had introduced me to the natural beauties of the Western landscape. The red rocks were the setting for the company. I was rooming with another dancer, Michael Smuin, and I was cast in three pieces: *Sinfonia*, *Nutcracker Suite*, and *Caprice*. You might be wondering if a new dancer being given the opportunity to perform in three pieces is typical or not. I learned new roles very quickly, so it became a normal occurrence for me.

I was partnering Jocelyn Vollmar, a ballerina of note. I felt somewhat sorry for her having to put up with this greenhorn, but she was very helpful and kind. When it came to the performance, it was thrilling. I did learn, during my debut, that dancers must be concerned not only with the quality of the dance floor or surface, but also the incline, if any, of the dance floor. I didn't expect the stage at Red Rocks to be slanted, but as I carried the *Sinfonia* ballerina on my back (we were back to back, and she had one lifted leg) across the stage I suddenly realized we were going downhill. I had to immediately adjust my pace and exert more control over my movements. Nevertheless, despite this surprise, the audience seemed to enjoy the performance. However, I don't know if anyone enjoyed it quite as much as I did.

At Christmas time, I performed in Lew Christensen's version of the *Nutcracker*, a very fine, very musical version presented at the War Memorial Opera House. I also danced in his *Beauty and the Beast*. Before *Nutcracker* season though, we had the opportunity to work with the San Francisco Opera as extras. We were paid five dollars for being an extra, a lot in those days, so I did as much work as possible, trying to save a nest egg for New York. I remember just holding a spear on stage and getting kicked in some very painful places. Even though I was armed, I didn't retaliate. I really enjoyed working with the opera singers, including Leontyne Price. Kurt Herbert Adler was director at the time.

When we were laid off for the summer, Michael Smuin, who later directed the company with Lew after his Ballet Theater days, had an idea to form our own dance program. We did; it was called Ballet 1960. He invited me along with Rocky Drew, Fiona Fuerstner, Paula Tracy (whom he later married) and some others. Mike choreographed a Vivaldi concerto and *Tris Colors* to Offenbach. It was the first time I wore white tights on stage. Ballet 1960 had no support except for the dancers and Michael. Mike was very talented and ambitious and clever. I believe he used me well in choreographing for me, and the reviews were wonderful.

I lived by now in an apartment that had been dancer Kent Stowell's; it had two bedrooms, a large front room, a kitchen and a large bath. I paid about sixty-five dollars a month. It was directly across from Golden Gate Park and the Japanese Tea Gardens, places I grew terribly fond of and visited often.

I was happy to be dancing, learning roles, performing, and living in a fabulous city, but the demands of military service began to encroach on my little world. After two years with the San Francisco Ballet, Mike Smuin and I believed we were going to be drafted very shortly. We felt we had to choose between being drafted and serving for three years, or enlisting in the Army Reserves. Since a multi-year commitment would wreck our dancing futures, we felt the Reserves were a better way to serve and preserve our dancing futures. We had seen our fellow dancer Kent

Stowell precede us (and survive) so we enlisted in the Army Reserves together in May, 1961.

I barely knew what to expect. Was basic training going to be as relentless and tough as we had heard? Was the food as awful as its reputation? Would the others think us odd and use us as scapegoats? We were soon to find out.

Though located in a very pretty part of the state of California, near Monterey and Carmel, Fort Ord was dreary and cold. The day before I reported, I had danced two performances of Balanchine's *Concerto Barocco* to music by Bach, and here I was, just one day later, on my way to marching through mud to the drill sergeant's harsh commands. No longer was I Frank Ohman; I was Br 1969981. For two days we received shots for more diseases than I ever knew existed. I did get some kind of an infection making it impossible to roll over in my bunk for three nights.

Mike and I decided to be army cooks, because we would have a decent schedule. As cooks we would work for twenty-four hours, and then have twenty-four hours off, during which we could practice. We planned to go to a dance school in the vicinity of the Fort to dance. The school's owner was nice enough to agree to this arrangement; we never saw her but she was always reliable and left us a key to the studio.

I kept reminding myself that Elvis Presley

had been here four years earlier and had survived, so it couldn't be too bad. It took me awhile to learn to sleep in a room with forty-nine other guys though. All the snoring—the short snorts, long guttural ones, whistles, the choking noises, you name it—made it hard to fall asleep. I found that getting to sleep first, before this a capella ensemble began, was essential or I was facing another sleepless night. In the barracks I repeatedly prayed that if I survived all this I would never complain about working and dancing. I think God was listening; he always has.

Staying in dancing shape was a challenge. I tried to work out during night watch. I sought the 3:00 a.m. shift, when everyone else was asleep, so I could practice. When I was sure everyone was asleep, and all was quiet and totally dark, I rolled up my fatigues, slipped on my ballet shoes, and did a *barre* outside, holding onto the railing. I must have been quite a peculiar sight in my rolled up fatigues, ballet slippers on my feet, doing *tendus*. Michael practiced the same way too. We had to listen and watch for the M.P., because when he came by for a night check, I had to quickly roll down my pants, shuck off my ballet slippers, and act naturally.

While dancing I was becoming known as a turner. Not wanting to lose that distinction during this army period, I tried to keep it up by practicing in the barracks. With one shoe on, one

off, I once did sixteen *pirouettes* on that tile floor
of the barracks. I am sure glad that Mike counted
and was my witness; I am not sure I was ever able
to repeat that number. While the other fellows
in the barracks were reading comic books, I was
reading about the lives of artists and sculptors,
like Bellini and Michelangelo. I did spend some
time in the canteen drinking a few beers and
listening to Ricky Nelson and Elvis Presley on
the juke box, a big change from Tchaikovsky.

After ten weeks of basic training, we were
allowed a short break followed by cook school.
In eight weeks, we learned to make baked items,
from biscuits to pastries. I learned to roast a dozen
chickens and cook sheet after sheet of bacon
on huge trays. But I think we really majored
in dehydrated food; there were powdered eggs,
dehydrated mashed potatoes, and foods that I still
cannot fathom being able to alter into powdered
form. I fell asleep during cook school with my eyes
open, a first for me, right on the bench. I think
it was due to bronchial problems arising from
the very damp Fort Ord evenings. On our breaks,
while the other guys were smoking cigarettes, I
tried to do push-ups to keep my arms strong.

I did make a friend in the barracks. His name
was Pick. We spent time doing latrine duties
together so we got to talk a lot. Though a quiet
type, he seemed to know about the arts. The others

seemed to take his name literally, taunting and ridiculing him, but I felt he was a nice fellow. At the end of the ten weeks, Mike and I decided to put on a show for the families coming up to visit. Mike choreographed it, and the parents loved it. It was at that time that I met James Dunn, the actor, whom I remembered from *A Tree Grows in Brooklyn*. It turned out that he was Pick's father, and he seemed to know of me. He thanked me for being his son's friend and not giving him a hard time like so many others did.

After the ten weeks, we got leave, and I hitched a ride to San Francisco. I was so eager to go back to this wonderful city, and I knew the New York City Ballet was performing at the War Memorial Opera House in San Francisco. I was excited about seeing Suki Schorer dance; she was formerly with the San Francisco Ballet and was now with the New York City Ballet. If I was lucky, I might follow in her steps. The wonderful *Liebeslieder Walzer* was on the program. I enjoyed the program tremendously. Going backstage after the performance to greet Suki, Mr. Balanchine and I passed each other. I was wearing my khakis, my army uniform. He nodded to me, as if he knew me. I was honored. I never envisioned that one year later I would be dancing for this company and for Mr. Balanchine.

From haute culture to not-so-haute cuisine, I returned to the base to cook chipped beef on toast for 250. I didn't mind my schedule as a cook, though I had to awaken at 5:00 a.m. to begin making breakfast. Hot cakes were a real favorite among the soldiers. All of us could drink as much milk as we wanted, and any leftover was thrown away at the end of the day. I was actually quite proud of my pies, though once, I was really embarrassed. I was in charge of making cherry pies for dessert, and I needed to make about forty of them. Everything seemed fine until the pies starting dripping, oozing, and running. There was no stopping this. Each slice became a river of red rapids, impossible to navigate with a fork or spoon, let alone devour. I had, apparently, forgotten to add the cornstarch to the cherry filling, an invisible yet vital ingredient. So my hungry audience found it impossible to ignore this mistake. Sometimes, I thought, ballet was easier.

It was a fine day in November, 1961 when Mike and I completed our Army Reserve Service and headed back to San Francisco. I was in quite a state, I felt; I was fifteen pounds overweight from eating Army food and not dancing, and I was to perform in six days at Red Rock. It was a pleasure, though, to resume dancing with the San Francisco Ballet. As a principal dancer, I was given wonderful roles. I performed frequently in three ballets of Lew Christensen's. I was a private and a lieutenant in his romantic ballet *Caprice* (quite appropriate casting after my recent stint); I was a dandy in *Con Amore* and a truck driver in *Filling Station*.

It was also here at the San Francisco Ballet that I got to learn and dance in some of Balanchine's masterpieces. I danced the lead in his *Concerto Barocco*, a technically challenging ballet that I adored. I was in the "Elegie" of his beautiful and haunting *Serenade*; in *Symphony in C*, I danced almost all of the male lead roles in each movement. On one occasion, I was dancing the male lead in the ballet's first movement. Unexpectedly, Mike Smuin had suddenly hurt himself and was unable to dance the lead in the third movement, and Lew asked me to substitute for Mike. So I ended up doing the third movement too, but the tricky part was doing the lead finales for both movements, simultaneously, at the ballet's close. An unusual position to be in, it all worked out fine.

With the summer of 1962 approaching, I realized that at age twenty-three, young in life but not in the world of ballet, it was time to try to dance in New York. A number of male dancers with the San Francisco Ballet felt similarly. Some of them went on summer hiatus and wrote terse notes of departure to Lew Christensen, but I was uncomfortable with such an approach. Instead, I spoke candidly to Lew, knowing that at my age this was the best time for me to try to succeed in New York, as he had done. It had been my dream and my goal since I was fifteen years old. Lew was very nice and understanding; he wished me well and told me I could always return.

When I first arrived in New York, I started taking classes at the School of American Ballet and with the Joffrey. The marvelous Diana Adams, New York City Ballet star, saw me and initiated a conversation, which concluded with her offer to make arrangements so I could take company class. Moreover, she generously offered to arrange a private audition for me with Mr. Balanchine when he returned from working in Germany. Now this was a highly unusual way of entering the company. The great majority of Mr. Balanchine's dancers came from his own school. So this was a rather unorthodox and stressful upcoming audition; everything I had worked toward and dreamt of rested not on performances over years but on one the one I was about to give for Mr. Balanchine alone.

How do you prepare for such an important moment? I suppose I have always believed that sincerity was an important factor. I passionately wanted to learn from Mr. Balanchine and dance in his company. Money or fame never motivated me. So, though I didn't plan it, my genuine desire to study and be part of this great man's company must have become evident to him.

Momentous occasions often occur in mundane,

ordinary surroundings. The first shy expression of love between a couple, for instance, may not take place in romantic Paris, or the top of the Empire State Building, but in a nondescript place that suddenly is transformed into a spectacular, illuminated paradise. Such was the case with the old School of American Ballet on Eighty-third Street and Broadway, an ordinary-looking building and studio. Yet, after I danced and chatted comfortably with Mr. Balanchine, it became exquisite.

Mr. Balanchine was very gracious and polite, with an aristocratic bearing but a wonderful air of informality. I felt immediately comfortable with him. Not only did I audition, but we talked, and I think he understood my sincere desire to be his student. It was easy and comfortable to talk to him, as if we were already friends. I had never felt this type of immediate connection before.

After I danced for Mr. Balanchine and we had chatted, I went to change and then went and spoke to the secretary. Mr. Balanchine was gone. In a clipped, efficient tone, the secretary told me to go to City Center for my contract and to head over to Capezio for my shoes. The enormity of what had just occurred struck me. After all my dreams, hard work, classes, juggling multiple jobs, and family sacrifices, I had just been accepted into the pinnacle of the ballet world Balanchine's New York City Ballet.

I had my skills, determination, hard work, and sincere dedication on my side, but I had none of the other advantages that people usually associate with this kind of offer. No, I hadn't taken class at the company's own school since I was a young boy, nor had I studied ballet since I was a young child. My family's resources had always been quite modest and we had no agents or other professionals guiding my career. Now, as with my parents and my grandmother in their own lives, my good fortune came about through hard work, sincere dedication to my chosen field, and perseverance. My grandmother's and my mother's lessons about life, which they exemplified so richly, were proven true in my own.

Chapter Five: From Rebel to Devotee

*"If (Balanchine) is to be compared with anyone in his
time in the frame of his own talents, visual or plastic
or musical, these must be Picasso and Stravinsky."*
LINCOLN KIRSTEIN

Mr. Balanchine then became my principal master teacher, in ballet as well as in life. Initially, though, it was all I could do to just get the basics right. When I joined the New York City Ballet in 1962, there were a major changes for me in location, colleagues, company, ballet techniques, roles, and so on and it took me a bit of time to adjust. The very first thing that I did when I joined the New York City Ballet was to go back to the West Coast. The company was going on to perform in Los Angeles, San Francisco, and then Seattle; a European tour, including Russia, would follow in late summer. So, my first class with Mr. Balanchine as a company member was at the Greek Theater in Los Angeles, not City Center in New York.

There I was, taking company class, my very first with Mr. Balanchine. And it really was first class. Looking around the room, I was awestruck. Was it possible that I was now in the company of ballerinas Allegra Kent and Violette Verdy? Was that the dazzling ballerina Melissa Hayden? And my movie idol, Jacques d'Amboise was I in the same class with him, too? When I had regained some of my composure, but surely not all, I gazed at the room. We were in the mirror-less basement of the Greek Theater, completely surrounded by crates of costumes, using portable *barres*. Mr. Balanchine worked with a group of dancers at a time; when they finished, he would take another group of about fifteen or sixteen dancers. If not in the working group, the dancers would stand around, watching.

Completely new to the company, not knowing a soul, I waited and watched during this first class. I was finally in the last group. I took a fairly innocuous spot (or so I thought). The incomparable Arthur Mitchell was just behind me. After class, Arthur Mitchell chewed me out completely and thoroughly. The gist of it, I rapidly discerned, was that a new company member, a member of the corps, does not stand in front of a principal dancer. I hadn't thought about this at all. Well, I apologized to Arthur Mitchell. After I did so, he eased up. Within a few minutes, Arthur recanted, telling me, "You will do just fine Frank, because you have humility." If I didn't have it then, I was certainly learning it very quickly.

Mr. Balanchine's class was challenging and he was completely focused. When I arrived in New York, I thought that I was a really good dancer. I could do consecutive double air turns (also known as *tour en air*), and multiple *pirouettes* (which is complete turn of the body on just one foot); I had danced the leads in some of Balanchine's most complex ballets, including *Serenade, Concerto Barocco*, and *Symphony in C*. Now, I discovered, I couldn't even do a *glissade,* an easy gliding step, properly. After my first class with Mr. Balanchine, indeed, I truly believed I could not dance at all. I kept asking myself, "Why did he take me? I can't dance."

It was a confusing transition in the beginning. Mr. Balanchine made us do more repetitions of everything and each class was different, focusing on one area. In my first eventful class, he worked on soft landings. I was self-consciously trying to land as softly and quietly as possibly when I suddenly heard someone behind me loudly saying "Boom, boom, boom!" There was my idol, Jacques d'Amboise, smiling at me, teasing me for my not-so-silent landings. This was something I had to work on.

In the beginning, after taking Mr. Balanchine's

class, I always felt I knew nothing. His technique was so different than anyone else's. I had had many fine teachers before, but Mr. Balanchine was different. He made us do more of everything. I was also immaturely impatient. Mr. B spent much time working with the girls in class, and this youthful cowboy wanted him to work with the boys. He usually worked with the girls first, spending the last few minutes working with us boys, but when he did, it was intensive instruction.

From the first I noticed Mr. Balanchine had an uncanny sense of what each of us needed to work on, but I never saw him act harshly or judgmentally with any of the dancers. Indeed, he never got angry with any of us. In casting his ballets, I observed, he always used the abilities of the dancers to present them in the best possible light. He knew how to cast for productions very effectively.

I started to get to know the company, especially on our train ride to Los Angeles together. At the outset, I knew Suki Shorer slightly, but no one else. I had a club car conversation with and got to know and respect one of the company's conductors, Robert Irving. When I was studying with Rozelle Frey in Los Angeles, we stayed after class one evening as there was a broadcast of the Sleeping Beauty with Robert Irving conducting the Royal Opera House Orchestra of Covent Garden. Now, here I was talking to him.

I also became acquainted with Pat Wilde, Jacques D'Amboise, Nicky Magallanes, Francisco Moncion, Shaun O'Brien wonderful talented people, dear friends all. It was all so exciting and new to me. I had previously read about so many of them; Francisco Moncion, for instance, was an original member of the New York City Ballet and even its predecessor, Ballet Society. He created leading roles in *The Four Temperaments*, and had created roles in so many great Balanchine works, and here he was, giving me his old theater case because I didn't have one.

Bob Maiorano was a very young dancer with the company just turning sixteen and his mother was concerned about her teenage son heading off to Los Angeles. He had grown up at the School of American Ballet, and had been Fritz and the Prince in the City Ballet's original performances of the *Nutcracker*. She called the company, asking whether someone could take him under his wing, and they told her that they had a new boy in the company —me— and that perhaps we should team up and be roommates. We did, and found we had much in common; among other things, Bob had lost his father too when he was very young. He helped me start my New York Dance Theater in 1974. We didn't know that we would become lifelong friends.

I wasn't the only new person to join the company

at this time either. Karin von Aroldingen, a former ballerina with the Frankfurt Ballet, was new to the company too. We joined at exactly the same time, along with Sofie Pourmel in Girls' Wardrobe.

The special talents I noticed initially in Mr. Balanchine, his ability to know his dancers, their strengths, and even their identities, were certainly at work in my first performance with the company. I made my debut in Todd Bolender's *Creation of the World* as a cowboy. How appropriate!

I was to learn that Mr. Balanchine loved the American West as I did; he loved the freeness, the spirit, the vastness, and the beauty of natural wonders like the Grand Canyon. He was quite a lover of nature. We shared a love of the Western landscape and its impact on its denizens. I have sometimes wondered if part of his appreciation of the vast spatial openness was connected to his appreciation of the United States' openness to innovation in art too, something he was unable to have in Russia.

While in Los Angeles, I was starting to learn roles in *Creation of the World*, and Jerome Robbins' *Fanfare*, and as an understudy for *Interplay*, but I was finding it uncharacteristically hard to learn corps parts. I think it was my resistance to returning to corps roles after having danced the leads in the San Francisco Ballet as a principal dancer. In fact, I think I had something of a mental block when it came to learning corps parts. I had never previously had problems learning roles, and I knew the lead roles of the very ballets for which I was now being taught corps roles, so I believe it was my own immaturity and frustration. I wrote to my mother, "They seem to think it will be slower with me, I believe... but later I will be something." I found out later that many in the company thought I had a block or learning problem; I realized, a bit later, what it actually was.

Even now, so many years later, I am embarrassed to reveal that I was late for my debut with the company. Busy talking to someone, I missed my entrance. It was inexcusable, and I never again did that. I think this unprofessional behavior was also connected with my problems adjusting to being a corps dancer. I was still smarting a bit from having performed lead roles and having received good reviews, and here I was in the ballet corps. I wanted to be dancing major roles; I had waited so long and worked so hard to be part of this company and I wasn't doing much after all. I stubbornly ignored the facts that I hadn't yet mastered Balanchine's techniques and style. Friends like Roderick "Rocky" Drew helped. Rocky, who went to the Washington Ballet, listened to my frustrations and told me, "Mr. B really likes you. You have to learn the corps roles first before he can give you other roles." Though this was rather simple, I wasn't able to see it myself and his words helped ease my adjustment.

When we came back to New York for a few weeks of rehearsal before departing for the European and Russian tour, I got an apartment right across the street from City Center. With help from Kent Stowell, a fellow dancer, I found a place at the Gorham Hotel on Fifty-fifth Street, which made it very easy for us to rehearse each day.

Before departing for Europe, I was still adjusting to class with Mr. Balanchine and his technique. After every class I asked myself why he had taken me into the company when it was obvious that I couldn't do anything properly. Yet I could see from the first how dedicated a teacher he was. I also began to see that the *tendu battement* was a key to his training. We had to do many, many repetitions. He taught us to shape the leg and foot direction from fifth position, outward. Timing was critical, and Mr. Balanchine spent much time talking with the accompanist about the music. The pianist played a chord, and we would do four *tendus* in between. So many other movements seemed to emanate from the proper *tendu*.

Mr. Balanchine, I found, would use some very different techniques to teach us. Sometimes he would take five dollar bills from his pocket, instruct the girls to place the bill between their thighs, and from fifth position, do *tendus* front without dropping the bills. To make sure the dancers used (and developed) the right muscles for turnout, he would sometimes pull on the bill. If it was easily removed, the dancer had to tighten the proper muscles.

Mr. Balanchine used other physical means to teach us his ballet style. Mr. Balanchine was my first teacher to use a rubber ball to show us the position of the hand and fingers. He had us place a rubber ball in the palm, using the thumb and middle finger to hold it. Many a time a number of girls would take the entire class holding the balls in this fashion. He would come around the *barre* to everyone and make corrections.

I was discovering that he used these methods because ballet moves are hard to explain. Ballet is physical, and he'd mention this point to us again and again. In fact, he often told us, "Don't be intellectual; ballet is physical." What I was beginning to grasp was this notion that learning ballet is doing it, not mulling it over and over and examining it at length. It is not that Mr. Balanchine wanted unthinking dance technicians; he understood that to learn as a dancer one had to do.

His other teaching techniques were equally valuable. He used metaphors or similes to explain what he desired; for instance, he used commonly observed phenomena to guide us, a familiar image that truly helped us share his vision and reach his goal. To help me (and the class) with my earliest of challenges, a soft landing, he explained that when we jumped, we needed to let the heel come down slowly, gradually, as if we were landing on egg shells. He explained that *developpe* (which is balancing on one leg and extending the other) should resemble the way an elephant's trunk picks us a peanut, in a fluid movement. Body position and *epaulement* were always stressed to the maximum; the shape of the neck should be rounded, as if a person was angling his or her face to receive a kiss on the cheek. His metaphors and similes created a picture of what we were striving for, and they were often beautiful at the same time.

Though I wasn't dancing many roles yet, I was learning from Mr. Balanchine's instruction. I started to recognize that he sensed my transition pains, my being perplexed at the way he did things, and my discouragement that I couldn't do anything properly. While sympathetic, he still wisely maintained confidence in his vision of ballet. He knew ahead of time, before most others, that his techniques worked. At one moment during this confusing part of my life, he told me in his gentle manner, "I might have a strange way of doing things with the company, but it works for me." His words helped me, acknowledging my being discouraged and confused while letting me know he had a bigger vision in mind. I felt his message, in short, was, "be patient, trust me, it will all work out." His intuitive intelligence impressed me. I had taken a leap of faith earlier in my life; I needed to take another now, having complete faith in Mr. Balanchine. It was the first time he had advised me personally. The nonjudgmental, understated, and very wise words of his were a hallmark of his instructing me about living.

In the late summer of 1962, the company headed to Europe for a tour that was to include Russia. This was a momentous occasion as it was Mr. Balanchine's first visit since his departure some thirty-eight years, and many dramatic upheavals, before. We were scheduled to perform first in Hamburg, Germany, then on to Stuttgart, Switzerland, Austria's Vienna and Salzburg, and lastly, Russia.

I had never been to Europe, so it was incredibly exciting for me. To be with this great company, this great man, George Balanchine, to be a dancer, to be touring abroad: I was overwhelmed with my good fortune and God's blessings. I remembered where I had worked, how I had scrimped, my mother's and father's sacrifices, my mother's unflagging encouragement, and my big dreams. I knew how fortunate I was.

Even the plane ride to Europe was exciting. Robert Maiorano celebrated his sixteenth birthday on the plane on August 29, 1962. On the flight over, I conversed with the great Arthur Mitchell. After our first unfortunate meeting (my usurping his spot in my first class with the company) he realized I was naive rather than aggressive, and so we sat and chatted on the way to Europe. Arthur told me I was humble, which he felt was a positive trait, and he was certain that I would be able to learn with this company. Later, in Russia, he wanted me to watch him in the first movement of *Symphony in C*, paying particular notice to when and how he pointed his feet. He wanted to show me, as well as get feedback. Here he was, a famous leading dancer, voluntarily taking the time to teach a little corps dancer. He also advised me to find and stay in a little European *pensionne* rather than a grand hotel, in order to save money. He was a wonderful mentor.

Bob and I did find a *pensionne* in Hamburg; we shared a room to save even more. The lodging we found was between two burlesque houses. This was quite appealing to the two of us. We were probably like two seamen who had come ashore after a long ocean voyage and found the allure of women irresistible. We were young, innocent, and adventurous, and we shortly found ourselves enjoying Hamburg's nightlife. So Bob and I explored Europe's artistic wonders and also a few of its feminine ones. Some of the strip clubs certainly got our attention.

Hamburg, like many European cities, had wonderful narrow cobblestone streets and buildings that had been there for centuries. Not dancing much yet, I walked back to my lodging one night in utter amazement after seeing a performance of *Liebeslieder Walzer*, thinking about its absolute beauty and ability to touch one's soul. A ballet in two acts, to music by Johannes Brahms, *Liebeslieder* is set in a grand house, with eight elegantly-clad dancers. Though without a story, the choreography is quietly brilliant. The dreamlike Act II, in particular, is imbued with emotion. I wondered how (and whether) I could ever learn something so beautiful and complex. It seemed beyond me.

What was easy was getting lost in this strange city. One evening I spent one and a half hours trying to find my way back to my room. I never had a good sense of direction. I couldn't stop marveling at the fact that I was with this incredible company, with dancers whom I had admired for years, on a European tour, when just one year before I was with my Army reserve unit. I was relishing every moment of the company tour. Just walking through the city, feeling the old cultures stirring, walking the paths as people had done for hundreds of years, was deeply thrilling. I went down by the old waterfront where Brahms, who was born in Hamburg, had played the piano to earn money and learn the music of the Roma.

On this first part of the tour, the New York City Ballet took all the ballets that were easy to transport as well as those which demonstrated the strength of the company. They included *Raymonda Variations, Agon, Episodes, Tchaikovsky Pas de Deux, Donizetti Variations, Serenade, Symphony in C,* and *La Sonnambula,* though there were others. I went to watch every night, standing in the wings to see if I could absorb the style and approach. I was shocked that the German audiences did not seem enamored with *Liebeslieder Walzer.* I believe they were disappointed with the singers, who were onstage with the dancers. So though this German tour was successful, we didn't do *Liebeslieder* again.

After our German tour, we stopped in Switzerland and then Austria. Switzerland was a beautiful country, and one of the highlights for me was the Zurich Opera House. Just as a precious jewel is set and showcased in a beautiful setting, the Opera House was set in the middle of a square, elegant and grand. A beautiful large poster of the New York City Ballet was on display in front of the Opera House, and it had Melissa Hayden in a *grand jete* shot from Serenade. Many of the posters announcing our tour had all of our names on them, and when we got to Russia, I saw my name on the same poster as Lincoln Kirstein, George Balanchine, Melissa Hayden, Jacques D'Amboise...I couldn't believe it. Sometimes

I still can't. How blessed and fortunate I was that this man had taken me into this company.

Geneva was stunning too, and the incredible beauty of the lake was particularly striking. Conrad Ludlow, Bob Maiorano, and I got paddleboats and went out on the lake. The birthplace of Mozart, Salzburg was also beautiful. I recall the Opera and the wonderful food and beer. Bob and I ate two wonderful meals in Vienna across from the Opera House and really splurged, because we knew our next stop was Russia, and we were not expecting superb cuisine.

I guess my time in Vienna mirrored my exploration of Germany. Young, immature, out in the world for the first time, I blended cultural exploration with the exploration typical of a teenager, I suppose. I went out with a German girl who I suspect really wanted to come to the United States and I ended up drinking too much straight Vermouth in a Vienna nightclub and no doubt clogging up my hotel room's sink for days, I presume, because I got so sick. Outside of a little Army drinking, I was unschooled in this too.

Throughout our tour, though, I took class every day with Mr. Balanchine. We did not have a practice room so class was conducted right on stage. As usual, he worked on specific things. Many times, it was correcting subtle movements or positions he saw during performances the previous night. He corrected movements that I believe the average to good ballet teacher would probably not even have noticed. Mr. Balanchine worked on coming through *pointe* and placement of the foot on *pointe*, so the girls always wore *pointe* shoes, never ballet slippers for class.

There was a young, tall, long-legged girl in the corps with whom Balanchine was working especially hard. I believe he saw her talent, once again, ahead of most others. Susie Ficker, later adopting the stage name Suzanne Farrell, was in the corps de ballet but once we reached Switzerland she was getting leading roles in ballets like *Concerto Barocco*. While her career was soaring, I was still stumbling.

I still couldn't do anything right in class. My eight *pirouettes* and consecutive double turns in the air didn't seem to matter to Mr. Balanchine. I was, though, growing accustomed to the format of his classes. Mr. Balanchine customarily arrived ten minutes into the class, expecting us to be completely warmed up and prepared. The *barre* portion of the class was generally about ten minutes long, and he didn't stress *plie* but *tendu battement*. The body needed to be challenged or it would become lazy was the Balanchine philosophy. Great repetitions were necessary so the body would not forget. After doing our *barre*, he generally worked with the girls on *pointe* or toe work, and the last part of the class he would work on jumps with the boys. Technical clarity was very important, and he'd sometimes focus on very specific movements. He knew what he wanted. He might spend an entire class on hands, for example.

Lest you think the classes were all intense, serious work, I must add that the soft-spoken Mr. B mixed anecdotes and jokes into his instruction as well. He incorporated everything he saw in the world, including food and animals, into his classes. Still feeling wholly incompetent, I was beginning to sense that Mr. Balanchine cared more that I tried and worked hard, than he did about my succeeding immediately.

Outside of class, he was patient with me about maturing socially. Like a caring father figure, he seemed more concerned about my character than my dancing. Though he had no teenage children he wisely knew just how to approach them, and in this case, me. Rather than blasting me with direct and critical lectures, a sure turn-off for adolescents, he quietly offered thought-provoking suggestions, and then left me alone to come to a personal decision. Ever so sensitively, he never spoke of such things in front of others, which would only have been embarrassing. Having carefree flings and escapades with women in Europe, my behavior came to his notice. It was on this tour that he began to speak to me of how women should be treated. He explained that women were special, "like queens" he said, and not disposable; they were deserving of a certain kind of respectful treatment. His words, his caring tone, changed my thinking about relationships.

Upheavals were occurring on a personal level at this time but also were afoot in world politics. It was a momentous event for George Balanchine's New York City Ballet to go to Russia for a number of reasons. This was Mr. Balanchine's first return trip to his homeland, having left many years before. Balanchine had grown up under Czar Nicholas II's rule, and Mr. Balanchine's graciousness, noble bearing, and fine manners reflected this time period. But he later alluded to the period of the death of the Czar, his family, and the ensuing revolution as "awful." His native country had changed dramatically since that time, and he still had a brother, a conductor, I believe, living in Russia.

Moreover, tensions were great at this moment in world history, as it was the height of the Cuban Missile Crisis and the Bay of Pigs conflict. The United States and the Soviet Union were on the brink of war. We got bulletins each day we were in Russia updating us on this crisis. The United States Embassy was stoned while we were in Moscow. Coincidentally, as our ballet company was in Moscow, the Bolshoi Ballet was in New York, appearing at the Metropolitan

Opera House. We thought that perhaps that was our safeguard; their company was in the United States; the American company was in Russia. Thus it began as a thrilling but scary tour.

We all stayed at the Hotel Ukraine in Moscow and had dinner together each night. Unlike other countries we toured, we were unable to sightsee freely. In fact, company member Shaun O'Brien arrived late for dinner one evening because he had been arrested for taking pictures in the park. He loved taking photos while on tour, and it seems the K.G.B. arrested him.

The everyday difficulties of life in Communist Russia were becoming clear to us. On leaving the hotel for the theater one day, a boy stopped me, demanding to buy my shoes, right off my feet. I explained I had no others; he was rather insistent and it took some time to get him to cool his own heels. The collective visage of the people of Moscow was as depressingly gray as the skies.

Our hotel lobby had a horrendous odor, reminiscent of malodorous, damp feet. A few company members wondered if their rooms were bugged. There was a choice of just two radio stations. We survived on cheese, yogurt, and bread (until I found a roach in the latter). Heaping bowls of caviar, though, were placed on the tables just as Americans would place ketchup or salt and pepper. Bob Maiorano was wise enough to bring peanut butter in his luggage, a scarce commodity in Russia, but the quantity was mysteriously disappearing each day, until we realized the hotel maid was surreptitiously nipping at the jar. I felt vindicated somewhat about my escapades in Germany because our actions were so constricted in Russia. One night a bunch of us got together for poker and vodka, but that was the extent of our fun.

We did go to the Bolshoi to see the second company dance a performance of *Swan Lake*. The sets and costumes were beautiful and the dancing was good but so very different from ours. They were more flamboyant but not as technically clean as the City Ballet's. Balanchine's style was unique and unmistakable.

Most unfortunately, Jacques d'Amboise had been disabled in a street car accident in Switzerland, so he was unable to dance on this part of the tour. Of the men, then, Eddie Villella, Arthur Mitchell, Jonathan Watts, Frank Moncion, and Nicky Magallanes enjoyed great success on this tour. Eddie Villella was celebrated for *Donizetti Variations,* repeating his solo after about twenty curtain calls. I had never seen that happen before nor since. The audiences received *Agon* and *Episodes* enthusiastically. Arthur Mitchell and Eddie Villella packed the houses. The audiences did not seem to harbor any political resentment toward us and adored the Balanchine ballets, so new to them. The ballets were taped during our Russian tour, and I am told Mrs. Krushchev came to one of the performances, so it continued to be thrilling for this newcomer.

My thrills were a bit vicarious though; I still wasn't dancing much yet. I did do Robbins' *Fanfare* (I was a tuba) and I was also one of the boys lifting the ballerina at the close of *Serenade.* Since I had done the lead previously as a member of the San Francisco Ballet, I did feel a bit disappointed and was so eager to do more.

At one Russian performance of *Serenade,* I was one of the four boys lifting Melissa Hayden at the end. I was unaware that the stage in Russia, like many stages in Europe, are slanted. The front section of the stage, that which is closest to the audience, and which we refer to as downstage, was lower than the back of the stage or that which is called upstage. Thus I unexpectedly had to walk up an incline while lifting the ballerina. More misery was to strike. Melissa's tutu (the girls wear long ones in this ballet) fell right over my face and I couldn't see where I was going. With her long tutu covering my face, I was virtually in the dark. After the bows, then, Melissa let me have it in no uncertain terms. "Honey," she said, "if you would quit working on those *tendus* and learn to walk across a stage, maybe you'll get somewhere." She chewed me out in front of everyone. Without much thought, I answered angrily: "I didn't work so hard just to carry you across the stage." As soon as I said it, I thought, "This is the end of my career with the City Ballet. I am going to be fired." One just doesn't talk to a great star, a ballerina of Melissa Hayden's stature, that way. I suppose it was my frustration with the limited amount of dancing that led me to thoughtlessly blurt out that statement. I am so fortunate though that throughout my life I guess God intervenes or has a plan for me, because what happened next was just what I was waiting for.

One of the company dancers left Moscow and the New York City Ballet rather abruptly. It was the only time I ever saw Mr. Balanchine let anyone go. This dancer was a heavy drinker, unfortunately, and would speak all too freely in what was a dangerous time and country. I think it pained Mr. Balanchine to dismiss him, but he was kind in giving the dancer his pay for the full tour, airline tickets, and so on. His misfortune was my lucky break; I was given his roles. I was writing to my mother throughout this time, and in one of my letters, I wrote: "Mr. B helps me. I feel I am being trained for his ballets, and the way he wants me to look eventually. I am improving very much under him."

A small digression before I return to the tour. Lest you think that Melissa Hayden despised me for life, or that in the next paragraph I describe how I was left in Siberia for my outburst, let me correct that notion. When we got back to New York, Melissa Hayden asked me if I would like to do a series of lecture/demonstrations with her. I had done nothing to earn this act of generosity. Abashedly, I surmised that she too was a kind and understanding soul. I was absolutely thrilled! We developed a fine friendship after such a rocky start. She taught me a number of roles and gave me sound advice at crucial times in my life. Years later, in 1973 when she gave her farewell performance, I danced with her in *Allegro Brilliante* and *The Four Temperaments* which I felt was a great honor to do. It was hard to believe she was retiring; Melissa was ablaze during her farewell performance.

On tour, I found the other dancers in the company to be true and so helpful. Arthur Mitchell wanted me to watch him on the monitor; he wanted me to see Bizet's *First Movement* and watch if he pointed his feet, a kind reminder to point mine. Later, when I did *La Sonnambula*, Balanchine's great dramatic ballet to Bellini music, Arthur was in the audience. He advised me not to look down. Pearl Bailey, he added, told him to keep his eyes on the front of the audience and the balcony, and to be certain the balcony audience could see the whites of his eyes. Good advice, I thought and remembered to use it. Offstage, my male dancing colleagues and I had pirouette contests that were entertaining. Regular contestants included Jacques, Bobby, Conrad Ludlow, and Earle Sieveling. We would start at three pirouettes, and increase as much as we could. It was great, sporting, fun.

Though our activities were restricted, nothing could dampen the thrill of being in the place where *Giselle* with the Soviet prima ballerina Galina Ulanova was filmed, a film I had seen years before in California. We were making our own history by dancing there.

We performed at the Kremlin Palace and the Bolshoi Theater. One day at the Bolshoi Theater, I found an empty studio and decided to practice my turns. A man peeked in. This kindly soul, probably a teacher whose name I never learned, gave me some excellent pointers on executing the step in Russian and French. I teach this correction to this day to my male students, and many years later, with my snow boots on, I did these same turns for Mr. Balanchine in 1983 in his hospital room. But while in Russia, I thought this bit of help from this anonymous man was unusually kind at a time when such heated conflicts existed between my country and his.

After Moscow, we traveled by railroad to Leningrad (now St. Petersburg again), where Balanchine had studied. Leningrad was cheerier than the very gray Moscow. One morning we went to see a performance of the second company at the famed Mariinsky Theater; Balanchine had appeared here in roles. The dressing rooms and corridors, I recall, had beautiful mirrors, velvet-cushioned lounges, and gold-lined interiors. We attended a *Nutcracker* performance; the staging and sets were incredible. The battle scenes had grand walls that collapsed; it was truly a spectacle. We viewed classes at the Bolshoi, Mariinsky and Kirov schools too. We also visited the beautiful Hermitage Museum, with its golden coaches encrusted with emeralds and rubies from the time of the Czars. I thought that might have been the first inspiration for Balanchine's *Jewels*.

In the Georgian state, we stopped at Tbilisi; this was Balanchine's birth place and the home of his brother. It was so different than the rest of the Russian states; the people seemed more spirited and outgoing. We saw an unforgettable performance of the then fifty-two year old legend Vakhtang Chabukiani in *Othello*. He was in magnificent shape, doing double character pirouettes and double *sauts de Basque*, a kind of jump in which the dancer assumes certain positions mid-air. This mustached, handsome man was a magnetic performer. With a stage full of dancers performing, my eyes were still drawn to him, Chabukiani, even if he was just sitting on stage. He possessed a rare type of charisma that I recognized again when I saw Nureyev.

Some of the grandeur we saw during part of the tour, which was created during a different era, was certainly offset by the living conditions and even the theater in Tbilisi, Georgia. It was a rather primitive theater, though the Georgians made up for it with their friendliness and invitations to join them for drinks. Though we were delighted to be here, we were growing weary and longed for our homes. Simple comforts, like having more than a mere hole in the ground to use as a toilet, were missed. We felt uncomfortably constrained; freedoms in which we partake without hesitation, like what we can publicly say, where we can go, what we can read, what we can listen to, were yearned for. The stress of being in Russia at the height of U.S.-Soviet difficulties was wearing, and so when our plane landed in New York, applause spontaneously broke out among the passengers.

Upon my return, I received a call from my mother who told me that the army had contacted her about my whereabouts. She told the captain that I was in Russia. She tried to explain to the astonished officer that I was there with the ballet, even at the height of the Cuban missile crisis!

The closeness I felt during our tour continued once we were back in the United States. I had nowhere to live when we returned to New York, so Ducky Copeland, the Company's wardrobe master, offered his apartment as a temporary dwelling for me and for Kent Stowell until we were settled. We did stay with this friendly, energetic and funny Englishman for about a month until we located apartments on Fifty-fifth Street. Ducky was always a very generous man in all my years with the New York City Ballet.

When we got back to New York, Balanchine advised me once again. We were backstage, and he was talking to me as a caring, non-judgmental friend would. With subtleness, he explained that the time had come for me to grow up. It was the time in my life to do so. Since I was so exclusively career-focused and self-supporting during my late teen years seventeen, eighteen, and nineteen my social development had perhaps lagged. So those annoying but developmentally necessary behaviors so typical of teenagers the rebelliousness, the risk-taking were occurring later in my life than was customary. Once I joined the New York City Ballet, and had reached my goal, I could indulge in adolescent behaviors I had postponed for so long. Mr. Balanchine understood my lagging in the area of social development, how it happened and why, and was extremely patient with me. Another might have warned me, reprimanded me, been highly critical, ignored my development as a person, or simply ignored me in casting ballets. Mr. Balanchine, fortunately for me, did none of these.

Instead, he talked to me of his philosophy. He talked about this existence as not being the only or real world but the shadow or spiritual world as being the real world. Life is more than just that which we see or are aware of. There was a higher guiding power, with a "third eye," he mentioned, who saw what was to come. This higher spirit, God, if you will, could look down and know that two unsuspecting people, strangers, were just about to meet on a street corner. If stopped before the corner, though, these individuals had no idea of what was just about to occur. From their perspective, they were just walking toward a corner, a rather narrow view. So though I was unable to see or perhaps share the wisdom of Mr. B's vision, I had to trust in a larger plan. This was so very like what my mother had always taught me, yet I had temporarily forgotten about what was significant and insignificant in life.

Later, thinking about his words, I realized that it was time for me to learn the parts I was given, to settle down, and to trust that it would work out the way I wanted. I realized Mr. Balanchine was unique in the manner in which he was advising me and in his message. This was not just about ballet. Quite soberly, I began to broaden my view of just my own immediate wishes and try to grasp the larger picture.

He wanted the best of all of us. Instead of

resisting corps parts and always asking, "Why does he do this? Why does he do it this way?" I began to see he wanted us to be the best we could be, as dancers but also as people. As he spoke to us in class and to me in moments alone together, it was clear that to strive for our best in every way was the goal he hoped we'd reach for, and his teaching methods were kindness, concern, gentle guidance, respect. Echoing my mother and grandmother, Mr. Balanchine was teaching and showing us that character counts.

While he was ever-aware of the spiritual plane, Mr. Balanchine was quite attentive to the physical world, the world that God had given us. He has been quoted as saying, "God creates; I only assemble." But he was highly observant and used what he saw around him. As aware of a spiritual existence as he was, he was simultaneously as down to earth as any in the company. He loved television, especially Jack Benny and *Gunsmoke*.

In the sixties, big company parties were occasionally given after a spring season evening performance at O'Neal's Balloon, across the street from what was then the State Theater at Lincoln Center. The restaurant was owned by the actor Patrick O'Neal and was a hangout for actors and dancers. There was a painted mural on the wall depicting the company's lead dancers. These parties would go on until the wee hours of the morning, but we would all be back in company class the next morning.

One time, as I was walking by O'Neal's, Mr. Balanchine asked me to join him and some of the dancers who were inside. Now he loved cooking and was really tickled when he learned about my stint as an Army cook for 250 soldiers, so when I came in, he began what became an ongoing joke between us. Mr. B said to me, "I heard you cooked in the army." When he asked me how many people I cooked for I told him 200 soldiers with another cook helping me. In the future, whenever he asked me that question I would say, "I can't just have a few people over; I only know how to cook for 250." He'd laugh, finding this very amusing. His simultaneous appreciation of the mundane and concrete and of the profound and esoteric was just part of his brilliance.

Classes with Mr. B continued, with his concentrating on specifics, but especially technical clarity. We might spend twenty minutes working on *port de bras*, for example. He had quite a sense of humor, often making a joke or comment about a current event. More than once, when something was wrong, he said, "Blame it on Nixon," since Presidents are always targets of blame.

It was still quite frustrating to me to try and learn his way of doing steps and integrating his techniques, such as a correct *frappe* or a *glissade.* I had to remember not to lift my toes and to drag the second leg. Yet I was asking myself "why does he have to do it that way?" less and less. Instead, in the evening, as I rested in bed, I mentally reviewed his class just before drifting off to sleep. Awakening to Mr. Balanchine's brilliance in life, and not just in ballet, I began to be fascinated with the artistic process he used to choreograph new pieces.

The first ballet I saw him create was the beautiful *Brahms-Schoenberg Quartet.* Amazingly, choreographing a new piece was a very fast process for Mr. Balanchine. In the studio, he worked so quickly, in part, because he had already selected the music and planned the ballet. Starting with the score, he had apparently already studied it and knew he wanted four boys in the first movement and so forth. He knew what music, the sequence, the number of dancers, and even which dancers he wanted before he came to the studio. So when it came to choreographing steps, he worked very quickly. Whereas in class he was very focused and intense, he was much more relaxed and experimental in choreographing. He'd often try different steps, seeing what worked and what to eliminate. Mr. Balanchine didn't write the steps down either; on the score, he just indicated entrances and exits for the dancers. Steps poured out of him. With *Brahms-Schoenberg,* he had Patty McBride and Conrad Ludlow in the lead roles, and most amazing of all, he gave me, the slowly-maturing newcomer, a role in the first group of boys. What insight he had, knowing this was what I needed, and what faith he had, too, believing that I was ready to do it.

And his generosity did not end there. He fostered my "conversion" from rebel to devoted student, from a rough-around-the-edges adolescent to a serious dancer and better person by giving me a major role in one of his ballets. The role that gave me a big chance and launched my solo and principal roles at the New York City Ballet was the lead in *Western Symphony*'s fourth movement.

FRANK OHMAN AND GLORIA GOVRIN, *WESTERN SYMPHONY*

Sure enough, before we had moved into the

New York State Theater just before Christmas, my name was listed to learn *Western Symphony*. This was a chance I hadn't earned but a sign of Balanchine's own faith. I wasn't going to let him down. Gloria Govrin taught me the part that Jacques d'Amboise had created. Jacques took me onstage and coached me too. And the significance of getting my first big break in a ballet that personally meant so much to me, given my Western roots, didn't escape me.

And so during the 1963-64 winter season, I performed my first lead and loved it. To add to this vote of confidence, just two hours before the performance, I was asked to do the first movement lead in *Ivesiana* too. Thrown into it at 6:00 p.m., I worked in an ultra-concentrated fashion and danced it two hours later. I overhead some dancers question Mr. Balanchine about why I had two leads that same evening, and joy and warmth spread throughout my soul when I heard his confident response: "Frank can do it." His emphasis was on his second word.

So here I was, doing the leads in *Ivesiana* and *Western Symphony*. My role in Western was quite an athletic one and one in which I could really allow all my passion and energy to pour forth. I understood the wide open spaces and that this ballet had to be danced that way. Mr. Balanchine always had a real sense of the West, the West that I knew. It was common to see him in a Western shirt and tie. We had talked about my childhood in that part of the country too. So his rare combination of understanding and interest in me as a person, of giving me a chance when I hardly deserved one, of sharing his philosophies about life, and of even selecting a ballet that was personally such a fine match for me, were profound gifts.

The next day I was exuberant. Mr. Balanchine never corrected the way I performed; he let me dance the way I wanted. And I danced Western with great enthusiasm befitting the part. Mr. B complimented me after I did *Western*, and in class, spent some time encouraging the dancers to project more, as I suppose I had done the night before. I bumped into the great Erik Bruhn this same day, and he asked me, "Frank, did you do something special last night?" Apparently he had heard about my last minute casting in *Ivesiana* and my doing the lead in *Western*, both firsts for me. To have this great dancer, someone I admired for years, recognize me for what I had done the previous evening, and to converse as a peer, a fellow dancer, was supremely complimentary. What a joyous moment, one I cherish still.

To my delight, I began dancing in other ballets too: *Interplay, Square Dance, Stars and Stripes*, and the second movement in *Symphony in C*. Without much preparation, I was thrust into the hauntingly beautiful *La Sonnambula*. Suddenly, appearing in only two ballets a night was an easy evening. I loved it.

During the 1963-64 seasons, the company was also invited to perform for a week during the summer at a major performing arts center in North Carolina. One of the center's directors, though, told Mr. Balanchine that he was inviting the company but added, "We don't want that black male dancer." He was referring to the great Arthur Mitchell. Mr. Balanchine, without hesitation, told them that if Arthur Mitchell did not go, the New York City Ballet would not go. So the North Carolinian retracted his ugly remark. The company went, and I felt fairly certain that Mr. Balanchine's casting of Arthur Mitchell in lead roles in nearly every performance that entire week was deliberate. Ovations were in order for Arthur Mitchell for his artistry and Mr. Balanchine for his integrity.

1964 was a momentous year, for the company and for me. The company moved into its very own home, the brand new New York State Theater at Lincoln Center. It was designed to Mr. Balanchine's specifications (though renovated years later). I was on the move too, renting a small apartment on Seventieth Street and Second Avenue, right over a bar. It wasn't a bad location to grab a beer before turning in for the night, but if I placed my beer mug on the floor of my apartment, I would have had to share it with the cockroaches which inhabited the place. I think they were larger than normal because they did a fair share of drinking. Turning the lights on as I came in the door would send them scattering all over the place. This was also the time that Jacques d'Amboise was choreographing *Irish Fantasy*, with Melissa Hayden, in which I had a demi-solo part.

I was deeply immersed in Mr. Balanchine's ballets. I was dancing an average of four ballets a night; I seldom had a night off. I was performing outside of the City Ballet too. I was doing numerous lecture/demonstrations with Melissa Hayden. She was great to work with, and so kind and instructive. The legendary Maria Tallchief asked me to dance with her too. What an honor. I had read her book years before, and now I was going to actually dance with her. We began rehearsing the Petipa *Nutcracker Pas de Deux* and Act Two of *Swan Lake*. I must say we got along beautifully; it was so natural to partner her. Sometimes she was a few minutes late for our rehearsals, and she'd come in wearing a fur coat and looking glamorous. I had heard that she gave private lessons to the young Caroline Kennedy.

I was learning that Mr. Balanchine wanted us to strive toward our best, and his best too. "A circle is complete," he'd say, "it is exactly 360 degrees not 359." So too was ballet, exact, not approximate, and we must aim for that. Yet never was he angry; he was always gracious. I was learning what he was moving us toward: a new vision in dance, an enhanced dimension in character. My life in ballet was joyously engrossing and strenuous and I loved it. I thrived on it; it wasn't a job to me. I had had jobs, like being a janitor, an elevator operator, a mail room clerk, and a lawn cutter. This was anything but a job. It was, to me, heaven on earth and it was not just because I was doing the sort of dancing I had dreamt of. Mr. B had become a father, a teacher, a mentor, a confidante, a genius, an honest person of integrity, a caring friend. I began to realize that I had a deep feeling for him, from my heart, and it had nothing to do with dancing parts. People were calling him a genius and a great choreographer; I concurred, but I add that he was a great soul.

We were a close-knit company. It was much smaller in the sixties, and we had fun. I was nicknamed Omanova, and Julia, because the guys were given their mother's name as a nickname. Although my mother's name was Irene, my fellow dancers said I looked more like a Julia, so Julia it was. Shaun O'Brien was Elsie, Deni Lamont was Alice, Bob Maiorano became Hope, and Earle Sieveling was known as Mitzi. Even Robert Irving, our wonderful conductor, was Ethel.

I was asked, as a regular occurrence, to dance

a role at the last minute, usually because of a suddenly-injured dancer. Such was the case with John Taras' *Ebony Concerto*, set to music by Stravinsky. How can I possibly learn this role, I pondered, when I'd never even seen the ballet?

In this instance the pressure was even greater because a dancer cannot be guided by the music when the ballet is being set to a Stravinsky score; the only way to learn it is by learning counts. Yet time was so short that there was no opportunity to learn the counts.

Tony Blum, a very generous dancer, taught me the role in the short time we had, and stood in front of me for the ballet, so I could watch him. During the performance, Tony kindly turned around to check on me. A critic, though, completely misinterpreted his actions. In his review, he inaccurately wrote that it was obvious that Mr. Blum didn't know the choreography because he kept turning around to watch Frank Ohman! I told Tony that I would gladly contact the critic and correct him, but Tony dismissed the entire episode, and we subsequently joked about it.

An elegant visitor came to watch company class one day. I was not very curious; after all, who could be more worthy of my attention than Mr. Balanchine? Perhaps I was really growing up. I had been told that a new work was to be set for the opening of the New York State Theater but this was not on my mind during class. The visitor turned out to be Antony Tudor, the eminent choreographer.

The next day I came in and read the casting announcement for the recreation of Mr. Tudor's *Dim Lustre*, to be presented at the opening of the new theater. "Villella, McBride, Paul...and Ohman" I read. A wonderful surprise. Rehearsal was scheduled for the next day with Mr. Tudor. The music, Strauss' *Burlesque for Piano and Orchestra* was beautiful. The ballet was set in the Edwardian England era, with costumes by Grace Costumes and sets after Eugene Berman. It was a masterpiece, I felt, though not well understood. It has psychological depth and resonance. It did develop a following at City Ballet. I was to dance the lead part for eight years, and its nuances had an emotional impact on the audience. Even years later, people would approach me and tell me how much it meant to them.

Mr. Tudor had me work with Mimi Paul, stopping us often during rehearsals to make corrections or suggestions. It seemed we never ran through the whole ballet because of the frequent pauses or interruptions. Mr. Tudor was quite interested in character; he took an intellectual approach to choreography. He choreographed to express feelings, and it was fascinating to work with him. I had many dinners with him at later times, and I enjoyed his company. He spoke of his life, his early days, ballet; we got along so well. No doubt, though, dancers needed good footwork to perform Tudor works. Hugh Laing, who had premiered the role in 1943 and had often starred in Mr. Tudor's ballet was on hand, kindly, and helped me learn the role.

After rehearsing this way, every day, for two months, Mimi and I finally danced in *Dim Lustre* the last Sunday matinee of the season. Unfortunately, I sprained my foot during the performance, but of course, I had to continue. It was hard to finish the performance but dancers have no choice. And then one of the most frightening moments I have ever had onstage occurred. During a momentary blackout during the ballet, a planned pause which occurs about midway through, Mimi and I both went blank. We hadn't rehearsed the ballet in full, without stopping, so neither of us knew what was next. Sheer terror possessed me. We were frozen. A few moments later, we heard the music. The music brought back the steps to us and I remembered Hugh Laing's pointers during rehearsal. We were able to finish, though Mimi murmured she was exhausted and my foot was throbbing by the end, and we had nearly forgotten a portion of the ballet. A near-disaster was averted.

Earlier that same day, I had been asked to dance *Episodes* for the evening performance in place of an injured Roland Vasquez. Though my foot grew to the size of a basketball by the evening's end, I danced the part in *Episodes*. After a week of crutches and whirlpool treatment, I headed off to Reserves duty at upstate New York's Camp Drum. Back to partnering mashed potatoes and wearing boots. But I felt differently about it now. I actually liked it, for the first time, and I respected the men who served. They were doing something important by serving the country, I now felt. Was it possible I was really maturing?

When I told Bobby Maiorano about injuring my foot in *Dim* with Mimi, we had a good laugh because he broke his wrist in the dressing room wrestling with Jacques. We thought that performing at the celebrated Jacob's Pillow Dance Festival would be out of the question for us that summer. Actually, I was able to go. Ted "Papa" Shawn was a famous modern dancer who had founded a dance troupe. Later, with Ruth St. Denis, they launched the Denishawn Dancers. He established the Jacob's Pillow Dance Festival and camp in the lovely woods of Lee, Massachusetts. Maria Tallchief, Royes Fernandez, Victoria Simon, Kent Stowell, Anthony Blum, and Suki Schorer were going to the Pillow, a group organized by Andre Eglevsky. Papa Shaun was so hospitable. I rehearsed *Le Corsaire pas de deux* with Vicky Simon, and afterwards, Papa Shaun said to me, "You have that beautiful soft landing of a Balanchine-trained dancer." What a compliment, and what a change from my very first class with Mr. B.

I had no costume for *Le Corsaire* but Royes Fernandez offered to make something. What a dear man. He went to Woolworth's, found some material, and fashioned a jacket, head band, and arm band. Walter Terry, the famous critic, gave us a nice review as did others. I certainly felt good getting a positive review but I never put all my faith in reviews. I thought the most important critics are the audience members; they decide whether it is worthy of watching or not.

Another highlight of the summer of 1964 was learning the role of Lysander in one of my favorite ballets and one of Mr. Balanchine's most beautiful, *A Midsummer Night's Dream*. This role incorporated acting too, so I closely watched dancer Nicky Magallanes. I was so proud and excited to do my first Lysander and with Patty McBride, too! We would dance together many times over the years and she was a complete delight: graceful, easy to dance with, and inspiring.

In fact, I was learning to partner from my partners. I seemed to be a popular partner for the ballerinas too, which was quite pleasing. Melissa Hayden instructed me, in her honest fashion, "Just be there when I need you, honey. You don't have to dance for me."

Others taught me how to make partnering more comfortable for the ballerina, such as the placement of my arms. A good partner, I was discovering, can spot small warning signs before something goes wrong, and invisibly correct it or avert a problem. If for instance, the ballerina's balance is a bit off or she is wobbly during a *promenade en arabesque* or doing *pirouettes,* I think it is the job of her partner to subtly, invisibly, rectify the problem, making sure she regains her stability. I always tried to let my partners shine. Too many male dancers I have seen are perfunctory partners, impatiently waiting for their variation. They are missing the joy of partnering. I always treated it like a romance, a lofty one, and perhaps not so coincidentally I was a sought-after partner. Partners need to be sensitive to one another, and must be able to communicate in seconds.

I once did the *Nutcracker pas de deux* with Maria Tallchief in New York. We had not rehearsed with the orchestra, so when we actually performed, we were shocked to find how slowly the orchestra was playing the music. It was almost slow-motion! Maria and I looked at each other, and knew what we had to do. Afterwards, she told me, "You are a real pro."

I was dancing regularly, doing new solo parts, leading roles, and my old corps parts. I was faithfully taking Mr. Balanchine's class and

absorbing his guidance. I was also involved for
well over a year, perhaps even close to two years, in
a relationship with one of the company's dancers.
Her desire was to have me study something else,
like business, to leave the theater, because she
was thinking of marriage, starting a family, and
having some economic stability. I had listened
to my girlfriend, and had given careful thought
to her wishes. But by the end of 1964, two years
after I joined the company, I had come to some
realizations. I made a commitment. Not to my
girlfriend and her plans, but to ballet and Mr.
Balanchine. I loved what I was doing; I felt I
was destined to do this. In what kind of state
would the world be, I wondered, if everyone
was a business person or a lawyer? I respected
these and other professions, but it takes all of
us including artists to make the world richly
diverse. I believed that God meant the world to
be as multifaceted as it is, with dancers, teachers,
accountants, physicians, musicians, and so on. No,
I didn't want to switch professions, or pursue huge
paychecks; I was exactly where I wanted to be.
I had started as a driven, impatient adolescent
who only knew his ultimate destination but didn't
comprehend the value of it. I now recognized
the meaning and value of my role and my
position. It was largely because of Mr. Balanchine.
   I recognized that Mr. Balanchine's ballet

techniques, his style, his choreography, were so far ahead, advancing this art form. More than that, gradually, without forceful indoctrination, I had come to share Mr. Balanchine's vision of ballet. It is hard to say when it started, but in Russia, watching the marvelous dancers, I had begun to see the differences. Ours was a cleaner, purer, faster style. And it went beyond these characteristics. I liken it to Mr. Balanchine having distilled classical ballet to its pure essence, its crystalline form. He hadn't stopped there, though. In a sense, he had also taken the language of ballet, separated it into its most basic elements, like letters of the alphabet, and constructed a new language of ballet, from these same alphabet-like elements.

Had these been Mr. Balanchine's only gifts, it would have been enough to make me fully committed to his language of dance. But his gifts were greater, and bigger. Making us better dancers, always working towards the ideal, made us better people. I believe to Mr. Balanchine the two were inseparable. He wanted us to be not just better dancers but to try to grow towards being finer people.

When he spoke to me of treating women as queens, as recognizing that God had a plan that we are not always aware of, that "third eye" he spoke of, or when he pointed out that what mattered wasn't really this earthly world but the spiritual world, the world where character alone matters, he was pushing me to be the finest person I could become.

I am reminded of some profound words of Jacques d'Amboise, who, many years later, at the time of Mr. Balanchine's death, remarked, "Mr. Balanchine opened up a window to enable us to see things previously unseen." He guided us to see a world of something better, not only for dance, but in life. His goal, to have us live the better life, to reach beyond what we were or thought we could achieve, was not at all limited to the stage. There was no real separation in Mr. Balanchine's philosophy, I concluded, between ballet and life. The way one lived his life, reflected everything he did, including dancing.

No, I was not going to become a lawyer or an accountant or seek my fortune or remove myself from this brilliant arena in which I was blessedly placed. I was no longer obsessed with getting bigger roles, or my rank within the company; what mattered was being close to this most brilliant of men, and being one of his students.

As is often the case in life, when one no longer pursues a particular reward, one is rewarded. The ballet I was completely smitten with when I first joined the company, and the one I was certain I could never learn, *Liebeslieder Walzer* was a ballet in which I was cast, in 1965. With gorgeous music by Brahms, a composer I had always revered as had Mr. Balanchine, I consider this ballet one of the greatest classical ballets of the twentieth century.

At first, I went to a rehearsal of the ballet, trying to learn by watching, but this was impossible for me. As Balanchine had taught me, a dancer must do. Melissa Hayden was dancing in the ballet and said, "Frank, let's learn it." She was wonderful and kind. Later, when Melissa was unable to dance in it, the delightful Patty McBride did, with Jamie Debolt. When he was leaving the company, rehearsals were scheduled for Patty and me to practice with Jamie. Both helped me enormously. It was pure joy and appreciation and incredible luck, I think, that I was now learning a ballet I once thought I could never learn.

I admit that I was nervous for a while in my *Liebeslieder* role, so awed was I by its complexity and its beauty. I wanted my dancing to be worthy of this masterpiece. My Mom came and saw me in this ballet before the company left for its summer European tour. She hadn't seen me dance that much and she always bluntly told me the truth. The latter is probably the reason for the former. When she saw me in *Liebeslieder Walzer*, she said, "You were a little stiff in the part. Loosen up." I like to think that gradually I did. I danced with Patty McBride and we did the last dance together. The music, the elegance of another era, the romantic nature of the ballet with its barely suppressed passions, all contributed to making it a very special role to me.

Not long thereafter, I was promoted from corps member to soloist. In the corporate world, formal announcements and press releases might be issued; celebratory events might even be held. The New York City Ballet world is different. My name was posted and then listed under "soloists" in the program. It was gratifying because of the roles I got to dance, and as a soloist, I could do other related activities, such as teach here and there. But the most gratifying aspect was to just be a part of this world of Balanchine's New York City Ballet. My mother, though, was absolutely thrilled with the news. She decided to come to live in New York. She got her own apartment, though she lived with me from time to time.

This two-month European tour held the same excitement for me as had my first, when I had just joined the company; and I was so excited about visiting European cities and locales I had only dreamt of or read about. But it was an entirely different experience now, because I was different. No longer the impatient, immature rather reckless young man with a teenage soul, I was more mature, contemplative, and philosophical. No longer was I thinking, "Wait until I show them what I can do!" and "Why won't they give me some roles?" but rather "I have so much to learn." I still felt those old stirrings, "I can't dance; why did he take me into the company?" But now they were a rarity. I now loved Mr. Balanchine's classes, still reviewing them before falling asleep each night.

Paris was first on our tour, and we were to perform at the Paris Opera House for a week. I was thrilled at the prospect of personally visiting and performing in such a legendary place, the location of *The Phantom of the Opera* and so many other classics. And here I was to dance in *Liebeslieder*.

Early one morning, before Mr. Balanchine's class, Bobby Maiorano and I decided to explore this place of mystery, the setting of such memorable novels. No one knew we were snooping about. We started at the bottom, going down two levels; the third had been blocked off. I knew from reading that there was even a fourth basement level, and that somewhere below they stored scenery. We traveled down the passages, seeing shadows, until we could look up and see the streets of Paris and people walking by. I believe the passages did connect to the sewer sections and underground river after all. Perhaps they really were escape passages from battles of centuries ago. How incredible to be performing in a place I had only seen in movies or read about in books.

Mr. Balanchine's classes though, were held upstairs with windows enticingly serving up the gorgeous vistas of Paris. The gothic gargoyles fortified the sides of the Opera House. The grand staircase, like the rest of the Paris Opera House, was beautiful in color and design. I was seeing the world while doing what I loved most and getting paid for it. I am so fortunate, I thought. For lunch, many of us would dine outside at the Cafe D'Opera just across the street, and watch in fascination as the sophisticated Parisians went about their customary activities.

Our engagement in Italy was equally wonderful. We took a beautiful overnight boat ride from Venice, Italy to Dubrovnik, Yugoslavia. We drank wine and dined. Dubrovnik at the time resembled a medieval city with its stone fortresses and cobblestone streets. We rented an inexpensive apartment that had the marvelous feature of being situated in a cove or lagoon, and we went swimming in the lagoon at night or day. We secured a boat one day and even rowed out to a tiny island, marveling at the beautiful churches and palaces around us.

A milestone of this trip was our visit to the Sistine Chapel. I was transformed the moment I saw the ceiling Michelangelo had created centuries ago. Its beauty was breathtaking; his genius undeniable, and the years of toil to create this masterpiece, impressive. Here was artistic genius brought about by extraordinary talent, vision, and endurance. I couldn't help but think of Balanchine. Mr. B knew that an individual's genius was the gift of some higher force, and not randomly or spontaneously occurring, like withered autumn leaves falling and landing haphazardly below. In this wondrous chapel, surrounded by such overwhelming beauty and feeling God's presence, it struck me that all genius was a gift from some higher power. Perhaps, I thought, this is one aspect of calling God "the Creator." One needed to be blessed in this fashion, and then use it wisely and well.

But even extraordinary artistic gifts from the Creator must be matched with prodigious human toil to see the realization of their fullest potential, as I was now seeing in the masterpieces around me. The parallels between Mr. Balanchine and his work and that which I was enjoying around me became vividly apparent. Developing one's talents to the fullest, working hard, being dedicated, having faith that it will turnout as one dreams, were the attributes to develop and live by. Mr. Balanchine had taught me this, in word and deed, reinforcing that which I had been taught earlier by my family. This moment of clarity, of insight, was transforming for this young man, a dancing cowboy from California, standing in the midst of the works of the artistic genius Michelangelo.

Certainly our tour wasn't all discovering world treasures or grasping elusive life truths, of course. While in Venice one afternoon, I was sitting in a cafe with other dancer friends, when

choreographer and company ballet master, John
Taras, the company Ballet Master, looking worried,
located us. Fixing his anxious gaze on me, explained
that I would dance *Agon* that same night with
Suzanne Farrell. "Go to the theater immediately,"
he added, "Suzanne is waiting for you."

Oh my! Could I learn it, in such a short time?
My mind raced. I had done the *pas de deux* in
lectures with Millie Hayden, and knew that well
enough, but learning the whole ballet with all
those Stravinsky counts was intimidating. Off
I hastened. Rosemary Dunleavy, the dedicated
stalwart of Balanchine's ballet mistresses,
was there to help me learn a few thousand
counts in the opening boy's dance and beyond.

Stravinsky is very hard to dance, because there is
no melody to guide the dancer. Instead, the dancer
must count, and each dancer keeps a different
count because of his individual role. To make it
more challenging, there are many, many counts in
Stravinsky ballets. When we were performing at
City Center, I had proven that I could learn quickly
and went on with minimal preparation in Ivesiana,
so I presume that is why I was asked to fill in for
Arthur. Well, we worked hard that afternoon. And
when the performance came, we pulled it off and
it went well. Suzanne was fun to dance with and
so dedicated; she gave 150% whenever she danced.
Suzanne was a good sport and a real professional;

it was one of only a few times, unfortunately, that I had the pleasure of dancing with her.

One of the most embarrassing moments of my career also happened on this European tour, but not onstage. One evening, I had finished practicing on stage and returned to the dressing room. Oddly, there was a mirror on the floor of the dressing room. I wondered, "Why is a mirror on the floor? Has it fallen off the wall?" I looked down at the mirror, and found it had been positioned to reflect the adjacent girls' dressing room. At the same moment, one of the girls saw me. Aghast, she scolded me: "Frank! You should be ashamed of yourself! Well!" I began to explain what had happened, but she wouldn't listen and clearly did not believe me. Sometimes I think there is nothing worse than being innocent and not having anyone believe you. Off I went to find some of my buddies in the company. A group of male dancers in the New York City Ballet were really devoted poker players, and I found them clustered in a group, playing intensely. When I asked them about the mirror on the floor, they shrugged, nonchalantly adding, "Don't know anything." That seemed rather suspicious. Nevertheless, I was stuck for a while with a rotten reputation, and the position of the dressing room curtain was altered so the real guilty parties could no longer enjoy the view.

When we returned from our tour of such

sophisticated, elegant cities, the epitome of the descriptor "European," off I headed to peel potatoes and scrub pots for the Reserve unit on Staten Island. I arose at 4:30 every day, got on the ferry, passed the lady in the harbor, and did my service before returning and reentering the world of dance.

As the year 1966 rolled around, I was again so fortunate and fascinated to watch Balanchine in the act of creating ballets. As a choreographer, Mr. Balanchine worked very quickly, knowing immediately whether something worked or not. He worked closely with the dancers while choreographing, yet the atmosphere was relaxed. It was breezier than class. When he taught class he was instantly focused; when he choreographed, he started in a much more informal manner. Often he'd come in and just chat. He liked to cook so he would sometimes talk about this hobby; he continued laughing at my running joke about my inability to cook for less than 250 people. In this relaxed atmosphere, we were all open to suggestions and willing to experiment with steps.

One of the small but significant showings of Balanchine's genius was his *Variations* ballet to Stravinsky's *Variations in Memory of Aldous Huxley*. Mr. Balanchine had studied the score, as was his custom, and knew what he wanted. In this piece, he took six boys, a corps of twelve women, and Suzanne Farrell, for the solo. The marvel of the creation of this piece! All three sections use the same music, but are choreographed differently to reveal different facets of the music. Though he never plotted out the steps beforehand, he knew immediately if the steps we tried were right or not. In just two or three rehearsals, it was finished. He had interwoven us in patterns. In this piece in particular, I felt he was using the same music for each of the three sections in order to educate the audience to a new world of ballet and reveal the music's nuances. Not only was he a teacher to us in the company, but to the audience members as well. It was special to watch Mr. Balanchine create. Observing a ballet take shape was like watching a growing cocoon that soon reveals the treasure inside.

This same year Mr. Balanchine also created *Brahms-Schoenberg Quartet*. I was fortunate enough to be in this ballet; I had a role as a demi-solo boy in the first movement. Gloria Govrin, Melissa Hayden, and Andre Prokovsky danced principal roles. As was his style, Mr. Balanchine choreographed this work quickly. His choreography was precise, simple, and beautiful. It struck me, one day, that being in this work was what I had always envisioned when I dreamt of being a professional dancer. The purely classical music of Brahms, the classical tights and tunic, the choreography: and I was in it! I believe it is one of Mr. B's greatest classical ballets, after *Liebeslieder Walzer* and *Jewels*. *Brahms–Schoenberg* became one of my favorite ballets to dance. It is romantic, wistful in parts, and lyrical. The inventiveness of the ballet is amazing. I made a recording in the dressing room when the ballet had its premiere. I play it often, in remembrance of Mr. Balanchine and of this beautiful work.

I was dancing quite a bit in the 1966 season and loving it, devouring it. Customarily I danced four ballets a night, up to about thirty-two a week with matinees. I learned to gauge myself so I didn't get hurt. Mom had advised me to pace myself appropriately, to carefully budget my energy. Typically, I would only take class, rehearse, and do a small warm-up before performing. Lincoln Kirstein asked me, one day, "Frank, why is it you are never injured like the other boys?" I told him I judged and planned my day by what I was dancing that evening. On days when I didn't dance much, which was rare, I took Madame Danilova's evening class. I loved these classes taught by a legend.

I never understood company dancers who did not take class with Mr. Balanchine. Not only were they missing his instruction, his vision, but they also missed his caring about his dancers as people. They were his family. He was so generous in working with all of us who were there to learn. No one, I feel, can teach people who aren't there to learn but just want to have all the parts and be stars, and we had our share of those in the City Ballet, but I feel they missed an incredible opportunity.

I am baffled too when I hear or read that some thought of Mr. Balanchine as anything but kind, even in critiquing our dancing. He was always trying to make us better, so he corrected our last performance but never in condescending, angry, rancorous tones but through suggestion and in the manner of a kind teacher. He didn't criticize the way I performed; rather, he would say "point your feet more," or offer a similarly constructive remark.

I never felt the New York City Ballet had a stranglehold on me. I certainly felt free to a great extent, to express myself and to do so through my dancing. I also was free to participate in outside activities. I know this contradicts others' opinions. I can't really find the evidence or instances among my memories to support the disparaging claims of others.

That year we moved into our summer home at the new Performing Arts Center in Saratoga Springs, New York. Some dancers put their names in the wet cement to stage left of the new theater. I imagine their names are still there. I didn't join them. I felt I hadn't done anything yet to deserve that immortality.

Our summer was relaxed yet lively. Bob Maiorano, Roger Pietrucha, John Prinz and I shared an apartment for a while in Ash Grove. I had just broken up with a girl in the company. I still didn't feel ready for marriage so I was as free and as interested in the opposite sex as were my apartment mates. Our interests were dancing, girls, and cards, in that order. We set up a simple system for harmonious apartment living whereby if we had guests we would leave a flag up outside and our buddies would return later when the flag was down.

In such bucolic, pretty surroundings, I began to write poetry and paint. Frank Sinatra or Liberace would appear in concert at Saratoga on Mondays, making it fun to attend. Gloria Govrin and a few others would go to see Marx Brothers movies. Even Mr. Balanchine was more relaxed, teaching class in sandals. He imparted that when I opened a school in the future, as he believed I would, I would need to educate the parents to the importance of good training in ballet. Good solid training was essential.

When we returned to New York, I got an apartment with my mother on West Seventy-seventh Street near the river. Mom and I could always talk heart-to-heart. It was nice to have her so close and she was one of New York City's biggest fans.

Lest you think the family's psychic abilities had tapered off, I should make clear that it wasn't the case. Mom and I still had premonitions, especially in the form of dreams.

It was around *Nutcracker* season that I had a dream in which I saw Roddy "Rocky" Drew, a principal dancer with the San Francisco Ballet and then the National Ballet, walking on a New York City street. Though it was icy cold in my dream's setting, he was not wearing a coat. Rocky wore only a lightweight sports jacket, wholly inadequate in the cold winter weather. I was struck by his unkempt appearance. In the morning I related it to my mother. Amazingly, when I went out that morning, my dream unfolded before me. I met Rocky on the street, a friend I hadn't seen in ages. There he was, looking a bit disheveled and without a coat on that very cold winter day. We spoke, and I couldn't help but ask whether he was OK; in fact, looking so cold and bedraggled, I asked him several times. He answered that he was fine. It remained on my mind; I kept thinking about the dream, then meeting him, and Balanchine's "third eye" that knows what is going to happen although we cannot.

Two weeks later, Rocky was found dead, his wrists slashed, in a hotel. I have always been haunted by this experience, surmising that perhaps my dream was an alarm, a warning sign that I missed. I've always felt guilty that I hadn't been sensitive enough to somehow prevent this tragedy. I should have done more, I have always believed; perhaps this tragedy could have been averted.

I continued painting, and started to give some works to friends and some to the City Center Department of Music and Drama to help with fund raising. One night, I signed autographs there with opera's wondrous Beverly Sills sitting next to me, asking to borrow my pen — a very sweet and humble artist.

Unfortunately, I also lost my wallet, which had about forty-five dollars in it. The following day, a boy called me, saying he had it and that his mother had advised him to return it. Though he lived all the way uptown, in Harlem, this fine young man traveled quite a distance to return it to me, with all the money and other contents intact. I thanked him, and gave him all the money; he deserved it. I told him, "You have been wonderfully raised. God will bless you all your life." That is truly how I feel about doing the right thing in life. God sees and hears all, and has a plan for us. Mr. Balanchine repeatedly stated that people would get what was coming to them, and that means good consequences as well as bad ones.

It was not my only encounter with Ms. Sills. In 1980, when she was the Director of the City Opera, Suzanne Farrell, Peter Martins, and I performed *Le Bourgeois Gentilhomme* for them with Mr. Balanchine's choreography. I had a principal dancer's dressing room to myself and dear Ms. Sills left me a *merde*, a good luck present on my makeup table. How wonderful was that!

Mr. B and I would periodically talk about life resembling a circle. We both believed that life is continuous and nothing dies but changes. I've always felt that lives connected with us in this existence can be with us in the next life, and like my mother I like to believe that there might even be a festival prepared in the hereafter wherein those who departed from this life greet us.

Mr. Balanchine and I grew closer not only because I was recognizing his unique genius but because he became a fatherly advisor. We talked candidly about women a lot and he seemed to sense when I was having problems with relationships. "We have to be careful with the type of women we get involved with," he quietly said to me. I tended to go to the movies more often when I needed to escape from my personal problems and I was going often and alone at this time. One day Mr. Balanchine commented, "They're going to run out of films, Frank." I hadn't mentioned anything to him and I wondered how he knew. He was just so much in tune with his dancers; his intuitive sense was so highly developed.

Much has been discussed about Balanchine and women, particularly his having been married a number of times, and always to ballerinas. Yet I never saw anything but a very courtly gentleman who placed women on pedestals. He remained friends with all of his ex-wives. I believe it said a great deal about his devotion when he took a year's sabbatical from ballet when Tanaquil LeClercq contracted polio.

When I think about him and his relationship with women, it is impossible for me to separate it from his life and his art. He was so utterly dedicated to ballet; it was truly his life, and women dancers were an essential part of it. Like paints, brushes, and models to a painter, ballerinas were his essential tools and his inspiration. I don't believe Mr. Balanchine to have been fickle or a womanizer, as some seem to believe.

As he so often told the company, that dancers learn by doing, Mr. B also instructed us through doing, not just through conversing. Over my twenty years with the Company, I was consistently cast in the *Nutcracker*, most often as the Father. Since the Father is onstage so much, it gave me the opportunity to learn every child's part. Periodically, I was cast in other *Nutcracker* roles including the "Spanish Dance" variation and the "Candy Canes" dance. Dancing a variety of roles in the same ballet was quite beneficial. Since Mr. B had predicted that I would ultimately teach, one of his teaching methods, I am certain, was casting dancers in different roles in the same ballet, especially one as large as the *Nutcracker*. His farsightedness enabled me, as a teacher and choreographer, years later, to mount the entire production.

Returning to the sixties, I was also thrilled in 1967 to watch the restaging of a personal favorite, *Slaughter on Tenth Avenue*. Ray Bolger was asked to help with the staging, and I had the pleasure seeing him at work. I peeked into rehearsals to watch Ray Bolger work with Suzanne Farrell and Arthur Mitchell. Mr. Bolger was recollecting *Slaughter*. Richard Rodgers was there too, standing by the piano with Mr. Balanchine. They were good friends. How blessed I felt to be able to witness this incredible talented group of artists at work.

By this time, I never missed a class; they were intense. I had so much to learn from Mr. Balanchine. The classes were geared to the understanding of clear technique and the beauty of the steps, not just the execution. I began to take the *pointe* class too, to better understand what the girls had to do, and sometimes I did more than watch; I participated, to strengthen my feet and my knees.

Inspired by Mr. Balanchine who continued to choreograph great works, I contemplated choreographing a ballet myself. I wanted to further expand my artistic impulses and express myself, if possible, in a new creative endeavor. More than anything, I wanted to prove I could choreograph as a way of demonstrating to my master teacher what I had learned from him. I was nervously excited. Would I be able to show that I had absorbed all he had taught me? Could I create a piece of such quality as to reflect the kind of teacher he had been? I did know the practical steps. He had taught me that to be a choreographer, one had to know the music very well, to study the score and divide it into sections, to choose the dancers, plot the dancers' entrances and exits, decide on solos, groups, and then start to rehearse. He taught me to leave myself open when it came to the actual steps, and it would take shape.

I once tried to choreograph by writing down the steps ahead of time and it was disastrous when actually performed. One needed dancers to try it out, to experiment, and to see the whole body. I learned these lessons about choreographing very thoroughly; in fact, I possess a photograph of a *Don Quixote* rehearsal held in the main hall of the New York State Theater of Lincoln Center. All the dancers, with the exception of one, are looking at Mr. Balanchine's feet as he demonstrates what he wants. But there's one lone cowboy cum dancer looking at Mr. Balanchine, and the position of his entire body. He taught me well.

Mr. Balanchine even gave me advice when it came to music. One day, during a rehearsal of *Liebeslieder Walzer,* Mr. Balanchine sat at the piano and suddenly played the second movement of the Brahms *Piano Concerto*. He played it without a score, and he was a tremendous pianist. When he finished, he looked at me, with his perceptive brown eyes, and said, "Frank, this should never be choreographed." He didn't elaborate. Perhaps he felt that the music is so powerful and so perfect, that it should remain as is.

Despite the pressure Mr. Balanchine was always under, from self-promoting dancers who wanted all the roles, to the financial and administrative pressures of running an arts organization, he still had time to be sensitive to my nascent choreographic yearnings. Thus when in 1969 I asked Mr. B if I could try my hand at choreographing a piece for students of the School of American Ballet, he was completely agreeable.

I had written out several ballets on paper that were terrible and I did not use. Ultimately, I chose Brahms' *Variation on a Theme* by Paganini which I now confess must be one of the most difficult pieces for piano ever written. I asked Jerry Zimmerman to play them for me as he had played them at his graduation from Julliard. Although he had asked for enough time to practice because of their difficulty, Jerry was wonderful.

I picked my dancers from the School, identifying those I felt had great potential: three gifted girls (later taken into the company) and three boys, including the young wonderful talent, Fernando Bujones, perhaps just fourteen years of age. Choreographing, I found, was not hard, and the project progressed quickly.

Mr. Balanchine, Lincoln Kirstein, Diana Adams and many others came to watch my first choreographic effort at the School of American Ballet. Afterwards, I waited to see what Mr. Balanchine thought of it. His kind words meant everything to me. He said, "Frank, you'll be a classical choreographer." No words could have meant more from this man who had come to mean so much to me. I wanted to please him, to demonstrate what I had learned under his tutelage, and I had.

When Suzanne Farrell left the company, Mr. Balanchine was devastated. He asked me if my mother knew astrology, and added that perhaps she could do his astrological chart for him. After all, he knew my mother shared his understanding of the ever-present spiritual elements in life. My mother was agreeable, and had me ask for some pertinent information about Mr. B, such as his birth date, and the time of his birth. She plotted his astrological chart, which proved to be the conjunction of three planets in Pisces. This is a very strong sign; it rules the arts. He was also on the cusp of Aquarius with Capricorn ascending. As a Capricorn with Sagittarius ascending, I noticed that we were somewhat overlapping. Mr. Balanchine held up two fingers on each hand, and said, "Look how we overlap."

My mother's reading emphasized that although someone whom he cared deeply about, had left Mr. Balanchine's life, he should not worry excessively, because she was going to return. My mother was unaware of Mr. B's personal life, so her findings were amazingly accurate.

His emotional pain was obvious though. After Suzanne's departure, he was terribly sad and often as he came into class I could see that he hadn't slept much. One day, he asked me to go to lunch with him, and we headed over to the Empire Coffee Shop nearby. Mr. Balanchine was terribly downcast. He was talking a great deal about aging and death. I tried to cheer him up, telling him that Verdi was still writing music in his eighties.

I knew he believed as I did that the physical body was temporal, while the soul was immortal, and the real world, as he had so often told me, wasn't this one; the spiritual world was the real world. Drawn into his existential, serious and contemplative mood, I began to catch fleeting glimpses, momentary feelings, about life without him, and the great void it would leave in my life. He had become my mentor, my friend, my role model, a father figure. So as we sat there, I asked, "When you do pass on, can you continue to be with me in spirit? Can you continue to be with me and guide me?" Mr. Balanchine looked at me with eyes that were so penetrating that I felt he could see through to my heart and my soul. He x-rayed my character. He must have looked at me silently for an entire minute, and then he pointed at me and said, "You will take my place." Tears suddenly welled up in my eyes. He was a blurry vision. I could hardly breathe. I didn't want to even contemplate, even for an instant, his demise. "No one can take your place," I answered him.

Ballet Theater was interested in me at this time. Ballerina Cynthia Gregory, a gifted and charming star, asked me to come to American Ballet Theater as her partner. Major gems were being dangled before my eyes: dancing with Cynthia Gregory, being a principal dancer, dancing major roles like the Prince. When I first came to the New York City Ballet, I might have leapt at such a chance. But a few years hence, I could not even imagine leaving Mr. Balanchine. After Cynthia asked me to join ABT, I asked her, "If you were with Mr. Balanchine, would you leave him?" There was a miniscule pause. "No," she replied. "That's my answer," I said. What could possibly be better than this? Leaving Mr. Balanchine was unthinkable.

From a self-centered dancing cowboy I had become a philosophical dancer and student, thanks to Mr. B. Many people viewed Balanchine as a very complex man. To me, though, he did not seem so. He has been rightfully acknowledged as one of the twentieth century's artistic geniuses, a great choreographer; I also consider him a great person. Yes, he was a true genius in the arts, but he was far more. A person of integrity, kindness, perception, spirituality, generosity, dedication, and loyalty all of these were aspects of this fine man. Had George Balanchine been anything else a florist, a chef, even a farmer he would still have been a great human being.

Chapter Six: What to Do with What I Have

"You must go through tradition, absorb it, and become in a way a reincarnation of all the artistic periods before you."
GEORGE BALANCHINE

If I were to plot my talents as a dancer on a graph, the years 1968 through 1973 would probably be the highest points on the chart. Between ages twenty-nine and thirty-four, I was at my peak as a dancer. I had been Mr. Balanchine's student for six years, and while this training had begun rather late in my life, it had been intensive. I now went to Mr. Balanchine's class thirty minutes beforehand so I was fully warmed up and mentally ready. I once calculated that over my twenty years with the New York City Ballet, I attended thousands of classes taught by Mr. Balanchine. In my two decades with Mr. Balanchine, I only missed his classes when I had to go for a scheduled costume fitting.

It was during this period of the late sixties

to mid-seventies, that I was not just a student in Mr. Balanchine's classes, but I became a student of his classes too. I hadn't planned it, but I naturally gravitated toward studying his way of teaching. I was observing and absorbing the structure of his classes, his teaching methods and style, and the physical training of dancers.

I observed that Mr. Balanchine sought to develop sleek elongated muscles in his dancers, not chunky or bulky muscles. His ballet dancers are taught to pinch their buttocks, hold the turnout, and use the back of the thighs or the underneath portion of the thighs for jumps, and not the knees or calves. It might surprise some to learn that it is the heel of the foot, and not the toes, ankles, or calves, or even the quadriceps muscles of the thigh, that provides the strength and takeoff power for dancing. The source of the power, then, emanates from the heel and continues through the back of the thigh. Mr. Balanchine's classes developed the light power in my legs that wouldn't have been there with other teachers. By light power, I am referring to developing strong but not overly muscular legs.

As an unofficial student teacher, I observed how Mr. Balanchine taught newcomers. He was particularly attentive to new company members entering the class, whether fresh from the School of American Ballet, whether tentative (many), or brash (some.) He corrected their *barre* work in his usual kindly manner, and focused on the movement of the legs and hands, especially the latter. He used his low-key sense of humor beautifully in the process of orienting new company members. After he'd correct a new dancer at the *barre*, he'd then ask them, with mock indignation, "Where did you study?" Of course they had studied at the school he founded and guided, but his remark would make them laugh and lighten the tension new dancers experienced.

Another key to his being such a brilliant teacher was seeing each dancer as an individual and continually refining that individual's technique or style. He saw what they needed to work on and knew their strengths. This was as true for the company newcomer as it was for the company veteran, like me. He tailored his instruction to the individual's needs. Knowing his dancers as people and as performers, he was able to astutely instruct, correct, and cast them.

Each class was like a unique small-scale work. It was a study, in the classical tradition, which magnified, clarified, and personalized his ballet precepts. I sometimes felt the same respectful hush in the room as I did in a place of worship. Nevertheless, Mr. Balanchine still made jokes and puns throughout class; his sense of humor was subtle and delicious. One of his favorite ways to be playful was playing on the sound of English words, words that sounded like something else, especially those with absurd meanings. When we had singers performing in *Liebeslieder Walzer*, for instance, one of the German words sounded like "mouse" so he'd say, "Here's the mouse part" and he'd get us to refer to it that way too.

From time to time, people have asked me for whom I danced while onstage. Is it for myself? My family? The critics? I have always danced for the audience, to entertain them, but when I knew Mr. Balanchine was in the theater and customarily he was I also danced for him.

As a seasoned performer by this time, I had developed my own performance routine, especially when dancing in four ballets each evening. In between ballets, I changed my costume and freshened up my makeup. I never talked to anyone during intermission; I wanted to stay completely focused. I prepared myself mentally for the next piece and my role. If the upcoming ballet was romantic or neoclassical or set in a particular historical period and place, I had to adjust my psychological approach to the role. In Toronto once, I went from dancing the lead in *Slaughter on Tenth Avenue* to the lead in *Dim Lustre*. I had to mentally transport myself from a tough New York City speakeasy to courtly, mannered Edwardian England in minutes, so absolute concentration was necessary.

While the audience is leisurely stretching or having drinks during intermission, behind the curtain is controlled mayhem. Carpenters are coming and going, stagehands are moving props, and wardrobe personnel are delivering costumes. So as not to get in the way of the crew, dancers try not to come down to the stage until five minutes beforehand.

By this time, though I had matured professionally, I was still finding my way in relationships with women. I was having affairs with different dancers. I was very attracted to the physical beauty of the girls. Mr. Balanchine, wearing once again the hat of a father figure, talked to me about it. He listened, and then thoughtfully said, "Spiritual things are the most important. You gain by that, not by physical attributes, or what you see before your eyes." He added too that sex without love was meaningless, unfulfilling, even base. My mother also continued to advise me about relationships with women. She was honest, and she was accurate. Career-wise, she reminded me to be loyal to Mr. Balanchine, though at this point, I needed no urging at all.

While my head was trying to understand my heart, the rest of my corporeal being was elatedly engaging in dancing new and established works by Mr. Balanchine and other choreographers. In the 1968 spring season, Mr. Balanchine created a wonderful ballet, *Trois Valses Romantiques* with music by Chabrier. I danced with Gloria Govrin. Melissa Hayden, Arthur Mitchell, Marnee Morris, and Kent Stowell were also cast in this six couple piece. The ballet was simplified the next year but was great fun to do. John Clifford created a piece around this time called *Stravinsky: Symphony in C*. I danced the first movement at a later time with Marnee Morris or Lynne Stetson. Johnny was always nice to work with; as a dancer, he could do about anything asked of him. He was a unique talent.

I regretted that I did not get to work with Jerome Robbins more, although I was in *Fancy Free, Interplay, In the Night, Goldberg Variations*, and *Fanfare*. I never danced, however, in *Dances at a Gathering*. My mother and I adored it. I'd have to include it on my personal list of the most beautiful ballets ever created. Jerry Robbins was one of the handfuls of choreographic geniuses of this century.

During our second trip to the Soviet Union in 1972 we were in the canteen at the theater having breakfast. Jerry and I started talking. I was honest with him and told him how smart I thought he had been with his career by creating a ballet masterpiece in *Fancy Free*, then going on to Broadway and choreographing several great musicals such as *West Side Story, Gypsy, The*

Pajama Game, and *Fiddler on the Roof*, then coming back to the New York City Ballet and working again with Mr. Balanchine. Jerome Robbins was a genius as well who worked so very hard.

In 1983 I was invited to the Kennedy Center to honor Jerome Robbins. We did a section of *Fancy Free* and I was the bartender. Jerry asked if I would do it and I was honored to be a part of his life like this. As an added bonus, during dinner I was sitting next to a most charming lady who reminded me of my mother. We ate and talked all night. I later realized that my dinner companion was one of the giants of the silent film era, Lillian Gish.

I continued to watch Mr. Balanchine choreograph, to explore the potential of human movement in ballet; at this time, he was creating *Tarantella* for Patty McBride and Eddie Villella. As he did when he was teaching, Balanchine truly had the individual in mind when choreographing.

He also had his mischievous side. I began to learn that when he was planning a surprise for me, he would avoid me. If we bumped into each other on the street in the Lincoln Center neighborhood, we always talked, but if he avoided me by crossing the street, looking away, avoiding eye contact I could be pretty certain he was going to surprise me in some way. During this time period, for several days, I believe, he ignored me completely in class. This was unusual. I was hoping that this sly fox was up to his usual tricks, but I couldn't be sure. Was he angry at me? Had I done something to offend him? About a week after he ignored me in classes, I checked the cast list for upcoming ballets and found he had given me the lead in part of *Allegro Brilliante* with the ballerina Allegra Kent, the lead in the "Five Pieces" section of *Episodes*, and in *Divertimento No. 15*. And Mr. Balanchine never said a word to me about it.

I was also getting better acquainted with Lincoln Kirstein during this period. He was a great, learned man of vision and accomplishment. Co-founder of the New York City Ballet with Mr. Balanchine, Lincoln Kirstein was always supportive and offered me advice and encouragement. He was quieter than Mr. Balanchine, and though highly educated and very cultured, he was unpretentious. I had first met and chatted with him when the company toured in Germany shortly after I joined City Ballet. One night we had dinner together, with John Martin, the critic, as well as Bob Maiorano. "These two boys are the future of the company," Mr. Kirstein said to John Martin about us. I was flattered.

So though my relationships with women needed some work, and my teachers in this area continued to be Mr. Balanchine and my mother, my spiritual life and my dancing life were soaring. Perhaps, I thought, my problems with women were meant as a means to learn some important life lessons, and as a test of faith. Patience and belief had certainly brought my dancing career to where it was, so perhaps I needed to have more of both when it came to women. Each joyous milestone in life, I believe, was a reward for the past or the present, yet again another test.

My memories of this period are filled with love. I was studying and working with people I had read about in the San Bernardino Library as a country boy with nothing but dreams of a career dancing on stage or in films. Nor did I ever envision that the great Mr. Balanchine would also be teaching me how to live. I understood, thanks to his guidance, that the question that challenges us all in life seems to be: What do we do with what we have?

Mr. Balanchine generously encouraged his dancers to dance as guest artists with other companies and delve into other artistic endeavors, like choreography and teaching. It was magnanimous and heartfelt on his part. With me, he seemed to always go about kind deeds in a quiet, behind-the-scenes way. For a few days in 1969, Mr. B avoided me, so I began to suspect he was planning a surprise as he had done before. Then Patricia Wilde asked me whether I would be interested in doing the lead in *Sleeping Beauty* in Atlanta. "Wow!" I thought, and then realized, "so that's why Mr. B has been avoiding me."

Indeed, Mr. Balanchine had arranged it for me. He loved *Sleeping Beauty* and he was planning to eventually set it for the New York City Ballet. Thus, after our winter season in 1969, I traveled to Atlanta to dance *Sleeping Beauty* with the Atlanta Ballet. All the peach blossoms were a welcome sight after a dismal New York winter; it felt like watching a glorious Technicolor movie after reels of black and white films.

In Atlanta, I took classes and did a full-length *Sleeping Beauty* with the Atlanta Ballet and the Atlanta Symphony at the Peachtree Center every day for three weeks, with six performances on weekends. It was strenuous but exhilarating.

So was dancing in *Sylvia Pas De Deux* with Carol Sumner, set for us by Andre Eglevsky, for whom the role was originally created. We performed at Half Hollow Hills High School on Long Island, after rehearsing at the old School of American Ballet at Eighty-third Street and Broadway. *Sylvia* was the hardest *pas* I have ever danced. There's an introduction, followed by a *pas de deux*, the solo for the male dancer, the female dancer's solo, then the coda. During the coda, at one point, the steps consist of six consecutive *assembles* and double *tours*, followed by a *grand jete* ending in a *pas de poisson* or fish catch, wherein the ballerina flies through the air but will end up on the floor, landing head first, unless caught by her partner. Her body bends in a fishlike arc, hence the name. *Sylvia* is packed with leaps and turns and requires great stamina and athleticism. What a thrilling challenge it was to do this ballet.

I also started dancing in Balanchine's *La Valse* at this time, and it became one of my favorite ballets. I did the third waltz with three girls. *La Valse* is dark, different, mysterious; the Ravel music is beautifully haunting.

It seemed like I was forever relocating. This time, Mom and I decided to move into the Ruxton Hotel at Seventy-second Street and Columbus Avenue. We paid three hundred dollars monthly for a front room, bedroom, bath and a built-in kitchen. It was close to Lincoln Center (and not situated over a bar) nor were its inhabitants largely or large cockroaches, so I was pleased. Mom lived with me until 1972 when she moved into the Longacre House for Women.

She wasn't bored though I was gone most of the time. She had a male friend she was seeing. I wasn't quite sure about him; he never completely gained my trust. I suspected he might have been only interested in her to get money from her. I knew Mom felt sorry for him, and she did help him a little. But I knew too that Mom was a person with high morals, and so perceptive that it seemed highly unlikely she would be badly used. Though her psychological x-ray vision had a fuzzier lens for men and a sharper one for women, I still had faith that she would eventually see the truth about him. I guess I was using Mr. Balanchine's technique of quietly guiding people while respecting their right to make their own decisions.

With a very busy dance schedule, it was hard but not impossible to keep up with my movie-going habit. In the case of *Midnight Cowboy*, though, I had two strong reasons to find the time to watch it. Dustin Hoffman was part of the City Ballet's extended family, as he had been married to Anne Byrne, a dancer with our company. He had been with us on tours and in the neighborhood coffee shops. We knew he was Anne's husband and an actor. About a year later, he became a major star with *The Graduate*.

Like so many, I always admired his acting and his selection of roles. He didn't just grab any part, and that was admirable (though it is understandable why some do). An amazing actor, Dustin was kind enough years later to come to the premiere of my company, the New York Dance Theater. Afterwards he told me he could have played the *Gershwin Preludes* on the piano for the troupe. I was so flattered he had come and said that. Had I known, I would have been thrilled to have him play, provided the piano was in tune, of course. So one day after rehearsal, having a rare evening off, Bob Maiorano and I went to see

Midnight Cowboy and of course, were so moved and impressed by Dustin Hoffman's performance.

Another highlight of 1969 was the company's Monte Carlo tour in June. This was a triumphant return for Mr. Balanchine to his post-Russian, Diaghilev's Ballets Russe de Monte Carlo roots. It was a place of astounding beauty. I understood how artists like Van Gogh fell in love with the region. It was so visually spectacular and unlike any place I had been, that I arose morning after morning after sleeping just five hours and sat outside to sketch the sea and the country before breakfast.

We danced in the Casino Theater, on a stage erected outside the Palace, in the open. The Casino Theater had small wings and indeed a casino in the front. Jacques d'Amboise was injured, so guest artist Peter Martins was asked to dance *Apollo*. I greeted him in the dressing room. Thereafter, we always had a joke for one another, customarily playing on the theme of being Scandinavian. Peter is of course Danish and I am half Swedish. Years later, Peter was very generous to me when I started my school. He taught a master class, and offered costumes and other help. Gelsey Kirkland had just entered the company too. In Nice, Sara Leland, Kay Mazzo, John Clifford and I took off along the Mediterranean Sea for Saint Tropez. The colors were unforgettable shades of violet and cobalt, framed by beautiful cliffs and rock formations.

Our return to the United States brought us back for our summer season in Saratoga once again. It was a lovely and relaxing time. Scads of jovial dancers invaded the local laundromat and dawdled at the local coffee shop. We got to the swimming pool when we could, though sometimes the girls in the company would get too much sun at the pool and turn a shade of cocoa by Act II of *Swan Lake*.

An onion, some free weights, a dozen or so ballet slippers, some worn, some brand new, tights, a makeup kit, a biography of Cezanne, a biography of Wagner: these were the contents of this dancer's theater case as the sixties drew to a close and the seventies began. The onion, which was sprouting without any help from me, came to be present in my bag thanks to the New York City Ballet season up in Saratoga. I guess packing up from the countryside I inadvertently took this item with me. This unexpected element in my theater case somewhat mirrored Balanchine's *Who Cares,* a departure from the Balanchine repertory.

The ballet, which he created in 1970, was a great surprise to audiences. Even the posters and the publicity were done on a larger scale than other Balanchine ballets. Mr. Balanchine was using the music of George Gershwin, whom he had met when working in Hollywood. I have often wondered, in fact whether the timing and the title of this piece, *Who Cares,* wasn't Mr.

Balanchine's answer to those biting critics who felt he was no longer capable of masterpieces. Yet even his process of creating this piece was different than his usual creative pattern.

Mr. B usually selected the music he wanted before choreographing, but in the case of *Who Cares*, Mr. Balanchine actually asked the ballerinas which music they wanted. Susie Hendl and I were paired for this ballet, so when asked, Susie suggested using "Do Do Do" for our *pas de deux*. Mr. Balanchine knew his dancers' strengths as artists and also knew them as individuals. He knew I had been a tap dancer early in my life, so he choreographed my piece in *Who Cares* to be more like an Astaire-Rogers dance than a classical ballet. Knowing my love of films and shows, Mr. Balanchine incorporated a bit of acting in my role too. This *pas de deux* is different than the other sections of *Who Cares*. Our "Do Do Do" duet was a great treat to dance. It was joyous and so free. Unlike other ballets, I didn't worry about anything going wrong in *Who Cares*. In other ballets, if a hard step was ahead, I was mindful of it. For example, in *A Midsummer Night's Dream*, there are a series of *pirouettes* in the finale that are worrisome. It is great if all goes well, but it doesn't always. The girls wear big tutus, which obscures the view of their legs, making it hard to partner with precision.

At other times it isn't the steps or the costumes

that can possibly cause problems in performances; sometimes it is just serendipity. In one mid-seventies performance of *Dream*, in the role of Lysander, I was lifting my partner during the finale, when my shoe got caught on the masking tape seams on the stage floor. I actually stumbled down onto one knee, but miraculously still kept my partner in the air. I was able to get back up too. Another performance of a *Midsummer Night's Dream* included a spontaneous siesta. My friend Bob Maiorano (in the role of Demetrius), and I had just finished our sword fighting scene. The characters onstage then fall into an enchanted slumber. Bob, though, genuinely fell sound asleep onstage. Talk about feeling comfortable as a performer! I had to really rouse Bob to get him up as we finished that slumber scene and the ballet proceeded. Bobby was teased constantly thereafter. Even Mr. Balanchine good-naturedly asked him why he had dozed.

In 1970 I had only the second dance audition I ever had, and again it was for Mr. Balanchine, when he was casting for the taping of *Slaughter on Tenth Avenue*. Mr. B came into the company class one morning and asked if any of the boys could tap. I raised my hand even though it had been thirteen years since I had my tap shoes on. When he asked if I could get them I ran to my apartment on Columbus Avenue and Seventy-second

Street and back to the theater with them.

Mr. Balanchine, Robert Irving (the conductor), and Gordon (the pianist) were waiting for me. Mr. B asked Gordon to play some of the tap sequences from *Slaughter*, and asked me to improvise something. I needed a minute and quickly worked out some routines that I performed for him. Mr. B stopped my routine and had Mr. Irving slow the tempo, as he said that what I was doing was very difficult. I got the part.

These were wild times for the country in the early seventies. Psychedelic music, outrageous clothes, hippies espousing an unconventional lifestyle, drugs and sexual freedom were all around us, yet these powerful winds did not deeply penetrate the walls of the New York City Ballet. Thus, when Mr. Balanchine choreographed *PAMTGG* in 1977, he incorporated an uncharacteristic nod to the turbulent times by including hippie roles. He formed the ballet's name in honor of a corporate sponsor and its advertising tag line, "Pan Am Makes the Going Great." I was cast as a hippie in this piece, and partnered Karin von Aroldingen.

Performing *PAMTGG* in Toronto, with Karin, I wore tight blue pants, which split during the performance. Oblivious to my ripped costume, I did my variation and as the dance required, sat or sprawled out onstage with my back to the audience, giving the ballet goers an uncensored view. I still didn't realize my pants situation until after the performance. Though savagely treated by the press, *PAMTGG* was just meant to be lighthearted fare. One of the Toronto papers wasn't fond of the piece either, but did mention that if I promised to rip my pants every night, then they'd enthusiastically support the inclusion of this ballet on the program all week.

The other intrusion of the times on our insulated world that comes to mind was an occasion during our Saratoga season wherein several dancers were arrested for smoking marijuana. The newspapers took note of it. Mr. Balanchine did take these dancers back into the company; they were not fired. Some other company members became regular disco-goers, and I went once or twice but it never really appealed to me.

Mr. Balanchine continued to teach and I continued to learn. When Mr. Balanchine worked with me, teaching and coaching me in a role, I had complete confidence for the performance. In the unrelenting August heat in 1970, Mr. Balanchine worked with Kay Mazzo and me at a two-hour rehearsal of *Agon pas de deux*. Though I had learned and danced *Agon* earlier in my life, there was nothing like having Mr. Balanchine teach a role. I watched him, his entire body, every nuance and gesture. What was extraordinary was that Mr. Balanchine taught a specific role to a specific individual. He did not present or teach the role as an inviolate suit of armor; rather, it was a dynamic one altered to suit the dancer cast in the role. Thus, in teaching me, he didn't seek to make my performance a duplicate of Arthur Mitchell's performance in *Agon*. The steps might be the same but Mr. Balanchine showed me I need not be the same cavalier as Arthur. Mr. Balanchine was brilliant in seamlessly integrating my strengths with the role without losing the virtuosity of the choreography or the impact of the work as a whole. Every point he made and each detail he covered was so vital and so enriching. Not a word or movement was superfluous.

Thus it was baffling and infuriating that over the past several years, Mr. Balanchine had been criticized for lack of enthusiasm and productivity. Some critics asserted that Mr. Balanchine's talents were waning. We knew this was preposterous. Such talk angered my Mom too. Personally, too, he was experiencing hardship, and I hated to see him sad and suffering. The critical attacks were a lesson in human cruelty and ignorance. Fortunately, Mr. Balanchine didn't really respond to criticism, nor did he respond to accolades. Remarkably, neither praise nor criticism seemed to affect him. "Why does it all have to be great," he'd ask, adding, "Can't it just be good?" It was another of his gifts as a master teacher. Through example and words, he never let sharp criticism, however stinging, nor high praise, no matter how flattering, alter his artistic mission. Instead, he was true to his vision, unaffected by capricious critical or short-term societal diversions. He wanted to create something lasting, existing long after the nasty words or fleeting trends had vanished. He knew the answer to one of life's central questions: what to do with the gifts he had.

We continued to have our quiet talks, and they were rarely about ballet, mostly about spiritual and personal matters. I am still so grateful for his deep, caring interest in me and amazed at his abilities to simultaneously care about others, create masterpieces, and run a company. Once, alone with Balanchine, I said, "I want to thank you for taking me into the company." It had changed my life. I knew, too, that had I joined another company, I probably would have moved on by now, perhaps to Broadway. I knew quite well that I was looking admiringly, even lovingly, at the reason I had stayed with the City Ballet. I did not want to leave the company because I did not want to leave Mr. Balanchine.

I also talked to Mr. Balanchine about my beliefs in reincarnation and past lives, explaining my amorphous feelings that perhaps it was in our dreams that we remembered our past experiences. We often spoke about loyalty and the human heart. Balanchine's genius had few if any boundaries. He even told me of an idea he had for a solar car. He explained it in great depth. He had insight into so many areas of existence. On one rare occasion, our chatting turned to the subject of ballet. "Frank," Mr. Balanchine said, sighing, "can you teach a men's class at the School of American Ballet? They can't turn." Of course, I was happy to comply. Mr. Balanchine had told me, after all, that I would be a teacher, and he helped me get started on that career, too.

Those who believed Mr. Balanchine's greatest achievements were behind him were proven wrong when in 1972 he created the Stravinsky Festival. Never in the history of ballet had such an extravaganza been undertaken. With twenty-two new works premiering over eight days, all paying homage to the genius of Igor Stravinsky, and the entire company, staff, choreographers, and crew devoted to this one gigantic effort, it was the first ballet spectacular of its kind.

As a dancer, I was in eight new works, including *The Song of the Nightingale, Pulcinella, Concerto for Piano and Winds, Danses Concertantes, Choral Variations, Requiem Canticles*, and *Symphony in Three Movements,* my favorite. Jerry Robbins was working on several new works for the festival, and collaborating with Mr. Balanchine on *Pulcinella* and they worked on appearing together in a short sequence. I had danced in Robbins's *Interplay*, a fun piece though challenging to perform, and in his *Goldberg Variations* and *In the Night*. In *Pulcinella*, I was a policeman. Mr. Balanchine and Jerry Robbins worked very well together in choreographing *Pulcinella*. To prepare for the huge Stravinsky Festival, the New York State Theater was dark for one week to rehearse, a risky venture but a wise one.

Trying to learn eight new pieces simultaneously and in a short time span was a challenge. The rehearsals seemed endless sometimes. At one point I looked toward my friend Shaun O'Brien and said, "What's next..." as I couldn't differentiate my right arm movement from my left. The Festival was the hardest I ever saw the company work in a compressed time frame. Most of us recognized that something very special was happening in the history of ballet; in fact, I think we knew ballet history was being made.

And indeed it was. The season was the biggest of the company's history and Mr. Balanchine became an undeniable international legend in ballet. The atmosphere of the entire season was supercharged. Excitement onstage, in the audience, in the ballet world, was almost palpable. The public response was wonderful and Lincoln Center was packed. Those critics with previously disparaging words about Balanchine's creativity were suddenly hailing and celebrating his genius.

And what about Balanchine himself? You might be wondering how he felt about this overwhelming success and recognition. Was he pleased? Mr. Balanchine was true to his philosophy. He was unaffected by critical words of exaltation or disparagement; their words, he felt, really didn't matter in the evaluation of his art. Among his primary goals was being true to his own artistic vision, thereby maintaining his artistic integrity. Moreover, what mattered to him was what he could create and pass on to us. To see the perpetuation and evolution of classical ballet was an urgent, underlying motivation of Mr. Balanchine's, his answer to his own philosophical question of what to do with what we have.

Lincoln Kirstein and I continued our friendship and we had many dinners together during the Festival. We talked about the company, ballet, and its future. He had written many books on dance and its history, and would spend some of his weekends at his Weston, Connecticut home. He needed a break, I felt, because he was always worried about the support and future of the company. A tall, stern looking man, no doubt attributable to his constant state of worry about the company's financial position, he was nonetheless a learned, fine man, with vision comparable to Mr. Balanchine's. He suddenly appeared on occasion to watch the rehearsal of a new major piece, but disappeared as suddenly, like a phantom, since he was always under pressure to have to fund raise and meet patrons or set up tours. It is amazing that he was able to write at all.

The year of the Stravinsky Festival, I left one of my paintings as a birthday gift for him. During the festival, he invited me to his Weston, Connecticut home, so I set out to meet him. His house was set in a heavily wooded area, and I went up a long driveway before I caught a glimpse of the comfortably old sprawling family house. Inside, there were old beams, plank floors, and potted plants all over. The house had a story, a history all its own, and a lot of character. Books were everywhere, the kind of old lovingly worn books that lured me to the nearest chair to briefly peruse yet when I next looked up, I realized that hours had passed.

On my first visit, Lincoln was writing intensely, banging out his ideas on a noisy old-fashioned manual typewriter. We spoke for a while. As we sat in the front room, an old car came down the driveway, and out walked Mr. Balanchine. The three of us sat and talked about the season, and how things were going. Sometimes our talks took a philosophical turn, but most often we talked about the company, just sitting there in the bucolic, serenely quiet, Connecticut woods.

Lincoln Kirstein's Connecticut house

became a refuge from life in the City. I visited a number of times. If Lincoln was working at his typewriter, I was free to wander, read, and relax. I often found myself reading something from his wonderful collection of volumes, but I also took walks by the pond. Here I could finally unwind and be alone with my thoughts.

Once the 1972 Stravinsky Festival ended, the company embarked on our summer tours that included Los Angeles and Chicago. We were also scheduled to return to the Soviet Union for our second Russian tour. We took the best of the festival's new works. How different was the atmosphere on this return to the Soviet Union. Our first trip had occurred when tensions between the U.S. and Russia were red-hot and poised to break out into a world war, so it was dangerous and unpredictable. On this trip, though, we were not in imminent danger of being trapped in a foreign, hostile country. U.S.-Soviet relations had become cool and untrusting though overtly cordial.

There was a Kremlin Palace party for the company and it was here that I met the legendary ballerina Galina Ulanova. I had seen the 1954 *Romeo and Juliet* in which she starred while in high school; it was unforgettable. Her eyes were meltingly beautiful as I complimented her that evening. Among the many joys of my dancing career is the pleasure of meeting people who have had such a positive impact on my life, and telling them what an impact they have had. It is wonderful to meet these individuals who measure up to one's mental image and do not disappoint.

The City Ballet had arranged for us to visit the Kirov Ballet's company school and observe classes and a school performance. I could even take photographs on this trip. The students were taught according to the Vaganova system, named after the great Soviet dancer and founder of the Soviet system of ballet education, Agrippina Vaganova.

The most noticeable difference between their ballet style and Balanchine's was the difference in arm movements. It appeared to me that Balanchine's techniques taught arm movements that were not only more fluid but were more rapidly executed. The Kirov, though, had a very clean technique that was not as flamboyant as the Bolshoi style. Their dancers struck me as a bit less flowing than Balanchine's, but ah, my bias is showing. Mr. Balanchine and I discussed the differences, and I learned that he long believed that Americans would make better dancers than Russians or for that matter, others, because Americans are such a blend of races and ethnic backgrounds.

I was struck with other differences between our first Russian tour and the 1972 trip. The change in me was unmistakable. Gone was most of the impulsive, experience-hungry, and know-it-all attitude. Now I was dancing a great deal, still savoring it, yet a hint of sadness crept into my contentment. I had reached my dancing peak, and there were probably not going to be any second summits ahead. Most likely I was dancing all the roles I would ever do. My momentary melancholia was offset though by a nascent interest in teaching. How ballet is taught, is learned, what teaching methods and styles and strategies are most effective, intrigued me. One evening, ballerina and friend Melissa Hayden advised me about doing work outside of the company, thinking beyond the City Ballet cocoon. "Do a little more on your own," she wisely counseled. I listened to her and I began to know, with growing certainty, that teaching was a component of what was ahead for me.

Odd things continued to occur on City Ballet tours. Bob and I were rooming together, as was our custom. One night he went out folk dancing, and hurt his knee. The local people suggested he soak his knee in vodka, and so he did. I laughed when he told me about this treatment, and suggested he soak his knee with hot compresses and drink the vodka instead.

It was uncharacteristic for me to sustain injuries but I did on this tour. I injured my foot performing in *Tchaikovsky's Suite No. 3*. Mr. Balanchine reacted with, "The Rock of Gibraltar is out."

Back in New York, with Melissa Hayden's

words ringing in my ears and my own intuitive sense urging me to plan for the future, I began to investigate the teaching of ballet and the choreographic process. I didn't really need to push myself; I was drawn to it. When I had free time I went over to the Library of Performing Arts in Lincoln Center and studied musical scores while listening to recorded music. I liked Beethoven and I often listened to his music or to Mozart's. Now when I watched Balanchine choreograph a piece like Brahms' *Schoenberg Quartet*, I would go over to the library and follow the score.

My first attempt at choreographing had gone smoothly, and it was intriguing and fun, so I began choreographing professionally when the Omaha Ballet invited me to do so. Valerie Roche, the Director of the Ballet, invited me and City Ballet soloist Lynda Yourth to appear as guest artists with the company. I asked Lynda if she had any favorite music, and she suggested Benjamin Britten's *Variations on a Theme of Frank Bridge*. This is the same music Lew Christensen had used for *Jinx*, his circus ballet. I liked the music and familiarized myself with the score. It was a dramatic composition, which hinted to me of a story. I liked the name *Deliverance* for my ballet, though my work bore no resemblance to the harrowing movie of the same name nor does it include banjos. I decided on a *pas de deux* with a corps. Lynda Yourth, a wonderful City Ballet soloist and partner, helped. I choreographed the lead for her and a *pas de deux* for the two of us. She was astonished at how quickly it took shape and said, "You did it so fast! And it's so good!"

Mr. Balanchine knew I was working on this project and in fact we discussed it on the telephone. He was generous in giving me the freedom to do this freelance work. Readers might be wondering why I didn't use music of Beethoven for my choreographic work. I have loved Beethoven's music all my life; his music overflows with humanity and is capable of evoking such strong emotions. It lacks nothing, which is probably why I have never chosen his music for choreographing a piece.

The bewitching mysteries of choreographing had certainly engaged me by the early 1970s, so I continued to do freelance choreography, following the creative process I had learned from my master teacher. I choreographed three ballets for the Boston Ballet while Virginia Williams was there and others for companies in Michigan, Ohio, and Maryland. In Memphis, I choreographed Gershwin's *Concerto in F* for a company.

In the early days of films and film studios, actors and actresses were under contract to the studios, having little say in what roles or in which movies they would appear. I felt so fortunate to have the kind of freedom Mr. Balanchine gave me (and others) to engage in other artistic activities. My Mom concurred, saying "he lets you go to get experience." My thoughts turned too to starting my own small chamber company. They could perform my original works. Though I believed teaching was also ahead for me, it did not seem like the right time to start a school. I was still at the height of my dancing ability in 1974. A school needs one's complete attention and time and I was still dancing.

I was concerned though about my future after I was past my dancing prime. I didn't want to become an encumbrance to the company, or stay on the payroll yet rarely dance. I spoke to Barbara Horgan, Balanchine's intrepid assistant. "I don't ever want to be a burden to the company," I told her, "so I want to try to choreograph." "You could never be a burden, Frank," she generously replied.

Mom, now living on Forty-fifth Street at the Longacre Hotel for Women, liked my branching out. She was also happy with her life, which was gratifying for me to see. Her apartment was in a safe area and she was near the Broadway shows she enjoyed so much. By mutual unspoken agreement, she saw me dance just occasionally, as she was very critical and very straightforward. She loved Edward Villella's dancing, and would sometimes remember to mention to me when she ran into Mr. Balanchine usually on Broadway

near the State Theater. They spoke as friends, and
their conversation rarely made any reference to me.

Since starting a school seemed unfeasible
at this time, I decided to stretch my artistic
abilities and try to form my own small
company that could perform my works
during City Ballet hiatuses. Friends advised
me to find an agent to represent the company.

Around February of 1974, I received a call to
visit Mel Howard Productions. Mel Howard's
office was in the vicinity of Thirty-third Street
and Second Avenue and we seemed to be mutually
compatible. He represented Bejart Ballet of the
Twentieth Century and other European groups.
He understood that the company could perform
only during New York City Ballet hiatus times,
and could not interfere with our New York City
Ballet performing schedules. Our discussion
led us to the topic of a name for the troupe. I
didn't feel the need to name it after myself; I had
learned from Balanchine that the ballet should
be the star. Mel suggested the name "New
York Dance Theater" and I happily adopted it
for the company. I also had my lawyer and
'balletomane' David Hoffmann incorporate the
company as a not-for-profit arts organization.

In many dance books and reference texts,
my New York Dance Theater is listed next
to the New York City Ballet, making my

heart warm to the close proximity of the two. The closeness exists both alphabetically and emotionally. I could never have started my dance group without the New York City Ballet.

In 1974 Mel arranged for the New York Dance Theater to give its first performance. It was time to select dancers for the premiere of my troupe. After announcements about the audition appeared in *Backstage* and other show business newspapers, about 150 dancers show up at the old rehearsal studio on Fifty-sixth Street and Eighth Avenue. With so many to audition, I was forced to make exercises at the *barre* very challenging to winnow the group.

I spotted a very talented Darryl Robinson that day, and selected him. A dancer of great stage presence, he later thanked me for helping his career. I also picked Christine Spizzo and Elaine Kudo, both of whom went on to have fine careers with Ballet Theater. Good friends Robert Maiorano, Lynda Yourth, Lynn Stetson, Judith Shoaf, Danny Duell, Deni Lamont, Janet Villella, and Delia Peters were to dance in this premiere performance and their talent and enthusiasm was a major reason that the debut was a hit.

We were in a frenzy of activity to get ready, though. Roland Vazquez, a City Ballet soloist, was the stage manager. Lynda Yourth stayed up until early morning hours sewing costumes. It was challenging to find the time to choreograph and rehearse for our premiere. A number of us were dancers with the City Ballet and that was our primary commitment. Once we were lucky enough to use the State Theater for rehearsal. Alvin Ailey popped his head in, looked around, and said, "Do you have any extra steps I could have?" I was always a fan of this nice man's fine work.

I was on the brink of another leap of faith. Years earlier I had packed up the little I had, and with big dreams, headed off to San Francisco. Now I was poised to take the leap from being a dancer to being a choreographer and director of a small company.

I was nervously excited about this double premiere: my dance troupe and my choreography. I had been so lucky to have the City Ballet's support all the way, the support of dancers and friends who wanted to help. I spoke again to Barbara Horgan, and told her, "I am not trying to compete with the City Ballet. I just need to have some artistic options when my dancing career ends." She understood.

Mel had arranged for our company to premiere on May 20, 1974, at Kingsborough Community College, in Brooklyn New York. The premiere went well, though there wasn't a huge audience. In August, Mel booked the company to do the Lincoln Center Out-of-Doors program. The program was a critical success.

I had created dance works to the music of

Tchaikovsky's *Variations on a Rococo Theme*, Brahms' *Piano Trio in C*, and Gershwin's *Preludes for Piano* for this. I was always touched by the words of Byron Belt who wrote in the old *Long Island Press*, "It takes a lot of guts for a choreographer to present an evening of his own works. Frank Ohman has the talent to match his nerve." I am inconsistent, I suppose, in heeding neither positive nor negative comments from critics.

It looked like these forays into choreographing and running a small troupe were well-received and promising. I seemed to have landed solidly after this leap of faith. As an artistic person, I had enlarged my arena from dancing to choreographing, and running a small troupe. Thanks to my master teacher, I had discovered the means to use what talents I had.

Chapter Seven: Unions and Departures

"But first, a ballet school."
GEORGE BALANCHINE

Whenever Mr. Balanchine was asked what a ballet was about, he answered that it was self-explanatory. Sometimes he'd answer by providing the length of the ballet, in minutes. I am paraphrasing Mr. B, but this is the essence of how he felt. He was not trying to be difficult or evasive. His neoclassical ballet's meaning is stated in visual, dance terms. Music explains itself. After hearing a symphony, few ask what it was about. So it is with dance. I found this out firsthand when I began to choreograph regularly. When asked to explain some of my ballets, I couldn't. The majority are plotless so they are meant to be watched and enjoyed.

In 1975 I was enjoying creating ballets, though the schedule was so frantic. Mel successfully booked us for a three week tour but we were in season with the City Ballet, with rehearsals abounding, and so it had to be canceled. In December, during our *Nutcracker* season, I was invited by the Boston Ballet to create a piece for their choreographers' workshop. I did *Melodie* to music by Tchaikovsky and it received some of the best reviews of the whole season. Though I mention the critical responses from time to time, and I have enjoyed the kind and appreciative words of some critics, I constantly remind myself not to exclusively rely on their words, except for a handful of very knowledgeable critics. I watched their fickleness with Mr. Balanchine and realized its unreliability. They don't really influence my creative process. Mr. Balanchine taught us to have a quiet respect for our work, its history, drama, and music. I try to hold to that tenet, though I am only intermittently successful.

1975 was memorable for the New York City Ballet's Ravel Festival and for the performances of my New York Dance Theater. It was also a time in this dancer's life, since I was age thirty-six, when I pondered how much longer I could and should continue dancing. I realized that I needed to seriously work on developing my company and choreography further and establishing a school at some future point. Would this be the right time, too, to settle down, to have a wife, a family? I yearned for that which I guess we all hope to have: a satisfying personal life.

For the first and only time in my life, unlike many of my ballet colleagues, I had to enter a hospital to have an infected (and neglected) knee injury cared for, but otherwise, life at the New York City Ballet was going smoothly. Mr. Balanchine was happy that Suzanne Farrell had returned to the company and he choreographed *Tzigane* for her. I was one of the four boys, and Peter Martins was her partner. It was good for all that she was back.

In *Tzigane* I got to dance with a lovely Nina Fedorova, a promising newcomer. Nina was tall with beautiful fluid limbs, and an exquisite visage. She made a gorgeous Swan Queen. I always thought Nina would have done wonderful roles in a memorable fashion had she stayed with the company longer. During the Ravel Festival I danced in *Daphnis and Chloe* with a new dancer, Kyra Nichols, who was lovely and impressive.

While we rehearsed for the Ravel Festival in the Main Hall, I was also rehearsing my troupe for performing in Italy and New York's Damrosch Park, both upcoming engagements thanks to Mel. We performed ballets from my growing repertory.

I printed 500 flyers for the New York Dance Theater's performance as part of the Lincoln Center Out-of-Doors Festival, and began putting them up all over the Center. They needed to be posted all over the city, I realized with growing dismay. How could I, one individual, manage to do that?

I shared my worries with my friend and New York City Ballet colleague, Bobby Maiorano. A mischievous smile spread across his face. "There's something I've always wanted to do," he said. He paused, gazing at me.

"Go on," I said, curious. "Let's throw them off the top of the Empire State Building!" he exclaimed.

"Are you crazy?" I said instantly, but then gave it a moment's thought. Could it work? Could we perform such an outrageous act without getting into loads of trouble?

We did it! We went up to the top level, the Observation Deck, of the Empire State Building. We each had about 250 flyers tucked into our jackets, and when no one was around, not even a security guard, we flung them over the edge! The flyers went soaring! They spread all over, carried by the wind gusts. I wouldn't have been surprised if some floated over to Queens and New Jersey.

When we took the elevators to street level, one lonely flyer came wafting down and landed at our feet. "Look at that," I said to Bobby, "it must be air mail." There wasn't another flyer in sight. We laughed all the way into the subway station. The performance, incidentally, was well-attended.

I didn't know until after the performance in New York that Mr. Balanchine, accompanied by dancer Christine Redpath, had come too. He never directly commented to me about it, but Ducky Copeland, who managed the costume wardrobe for Mr. Balanchine, asked me for the costumes used in the performance. He had them all cleaned, at Mr. Balanchine's insistence. The sly fox was at it again. After the excitement of the Ravel Festival, the New York Dance Theater accepted an invitation to perform at Italy's Venice Festival and to perform at Parma and Lac de Garde. The programs would consist of all my own pieces, some new and some re-creations. We were received very well. Since Parma is a city with a long passionate romance with opera, I used Wagner's *Tristan und Isolde* and it was popular with the audiences. The dancers were showered with "Bravos." My friend Robert Maiorano unfortunately hurt his foot, rendering him unable to dance Soliloquy, which I had choreographed to Britten's *Serenade for Tenor, Horn, and Strings* for him. I had to go on in all of his parts. Two other dancers had to leave Europe, but otherwise, the tour fared well.

In August of 1976, my wishes were once again granted when our Delacourt Theater performance, in Central Park, was met with great reviews and ovations. The program included a twenty minute classical ballet to Johannes Brahms' *Violin Romanzen*. What a joy to use music I had always loved since the time I snuck library records into my California bedroom.

I used ten dedicated dancers for this performance, all receiving a paltry forty-five dollars apiece. I felt terrible that I could not even offer them rehearsal pay, but they never complained. Lynda Yourth was one of the dancers and also our costumer. She was talented at design, and could take a Simplicity pattern and fashion a costume from it. Judy Shoaff, Bob Maiorano, Elaine Bauer, David Brown, and Darryl Robinson were among our talented dancers. The New York papers reviewed the performance and gave us good notices. My toughest critic my mother came too, and was delighted with it.

Though we never directly talked about the New York Dance Theater's Park performance, Mr. Balanchine and I communicated closely as we always had. He asked me, "Are you staging things?" I said "yes," and I explained that I set a short piece, *Hoedown* to a popular Arthur Fiedler medley, an homage to his *Western Symphony*.

Sometimes I talked to Mr. Balanchine about music. Once I wanted his opinion about using Tchaikovsky's *Rococo Variations for Cello and Orchestra*, and he said, "It's a bit scratchy, dear." He told me to do something to Donizetti instead. Mr. Balanchine explained to me that one had to create at least ten ballets to make one that is worthwhile. When I thought about the pieces I had choreographed, I had to greatly inflate the number of creations just to come close to one.

Mr. Balanchine, meanwhile, continued creating, never satisfied to pause or rest on his body of masterpieces. In fact, he never liked to look back. Once, when asked about his past, the Diaghilev period I believe, Mr. Balanchine replied that people who live in the past are unhappy people. He felt we must all live in the present, live now. His wise words echoed those of my grandmother, who remembered the past but lived in the present.

I had no idea at this time that Mr. Balanchine's health was not strong. He was always there for us, always demonstrating the same consistent dedication. We would often stop and talk on the streets surrounding Lincoln Center. He'd still show his mischievous side from time to time too. I knew his pattern. If he was walking across the street and deliberately averted his eyes so as not to make eye contact with me, I'd chuckle and tell myself, "He's up to something." And then a day or two later he'd spring a surprise on me.

Only once do I recall meeting a weary Mr. Balanchine in front of the theater. He commented, "I have to get away for some peace and quiet." He was going to Switzerland, where he was thinking of starting a new company in Geneva.

Examining the contents of my ballet case at this point would have turned up a dancer's usual collection of shoes, stage makeup, and tights. As a budding choreographer, my case also contained musical scores, travel schedules for visiting other companies to set ballets, and hastily scribbled ideas for the New York Dance Theater. Noticeably absent from my ballet case were photographs of a romantic partner, but that was about to change.

I was invited to set a ballet for Gloria Isaksen, director of her own school and company, the Potomac Ballet in Maryland. I sent her music, a Chopin *Trio* that I planned to use for a new ballet for her troupe. Gloria lived with her parents, who kindly invited me to stay with them while I was working for her school and company. It was fun to work there; it was a nice break from the stressful and too hectic pace of life in New York. A comfortable closeness was starting to develop between us and it was different than anything I had experienced earlier in my life.

It was hot that Bicentennial summer; the amazing athlete Nadia Comaneci scored a perfect ten in the Olympics. Gloria and I were getting closer. Gloria too had some Scandinavian blood; her father was part Norwegian. A small, pretty blond, she was soft-spoken and quiet by nature. She had danced with the Pennsylvania Ballet and at Radio City before starting her school and company. I kept going back to Maryland just to help her, I initially told myself, and we grew closer and more and more fond of one another. In a lucky turn of events, the male dancer I had planned to use in the Chopin piece for her company dropped out. Though I had another well-paying engagement, I cancelled it and told myself I had to fill in myself, because I had promised Gloria. This was not the truth, though; I was really enamored with Gloria. So I told her I would dance this new piece with her.

Dancing with someone you are dating is quite romantic; it is another form of courtship. Over the next year and a half, I started commuting to Maryland regularly, whenever I wasn't performing with the City Ballet or engaged in New York Dance Theater business.

While Gloria and I were dating, though, the Company had a musician's strike that lasted six weeks, so we were laid off. Mr. Balanchine, always looking out for his dancers, gave us work by having dances filmed for the Performing Arts Library, enabling us to continue to receive paychecks. I had a great time dancing with Marnee Morris in *Symphony in C.*

Because of the way I felt about Balanchine, I had never been interested in parting company from his troupe. He never gave me the slightest nudge, push, or shove out of the New York City Ballet, even when I was no longer at my peak as a dancer. Nevertheless, I felt somewhat guilty if I were to hang on without making any kind of important contribution.

I wanted to teach the ballet of Balanchine, and this seemed like a noble goal for my post-City Ballet years. The freelance choreography and the New York Dance Theater were all going to be important parts of my post-dancing life. A school, like Gloria's, I reasoned, was important and once I retired from dancing I could devote the daily hours needed to establish and build a school. I knew the school's foundation would be the teaching of ballet in the Balanchine tradition; that was its mission. I knew it was wise to stay around the New York metropolitan area because it is such a hub of dance activity. But where to establish it?

Once again, I felt I needed Mr. Balanchine's advice, this time, with regard to the location of a school. "Where would it be best to establish a school," I asked, "Long Island or Connecticut?" Mr. Balanchine advised me that Long Island was a better choice. He reminded me that he had a home in Fort Salonga when he was married to Vera Zorina. His impression of Connecticut, he said, was a state with many big cities which had a full array of ballet companies and schools; Long Island, he added, had only the Eglevsky School and Company as a serious place to train. I did not hesitate to accept his advice.

With all of my activities New York City Ballet dancing, choreographing, dating an out-of-state woman, guiding the New York Dance

Theater coupled with Mr. Balanchine's always overwhelming schedule and responsibilities, it is amazing that we found moments for fun too. I had a funny costume for my role in the second act of Mr. B's *Don Quixote*. Mr. B always liked to make a comment about my hat, especially the feather. To him, it looked like it was backwards, and we had a running joke about this garment. "Frank, your hat is backwards," he'd always call after me. I never tired of hearing him say it time after time. I looked forward to his remark.

Balanchine continued to create and made *Union Jack* just as quickly as he had so many other ballets. The finale had about seventy of us (many who were in earlier parts of the ballet) rehearsing together in the main hall; it was so much fun to do.

In 1977, with an eye toward my post-dancing years, I accepted a great challenge by accepting the Directorship of the Syracuse New York ballet. I looked forward to choreographing new works, resetting others, and carrying out my creative vision, solidly rooted in the Balanchine tradition. Over the next several months, I set about ten ballets with the company. One major work was a ballet to Dvorak's *New World Symphony*. This was a major undertaking and my biggest one, until I did *Nutcracker* and *Lisa* in more recent years. It directly followed on the heels of my teaching and staging three of my own ballets at Indiana University

School of Music, where my friend Marina Svetlova was now Chairwoman of the Dance Department. Marina has been a wonderful friend for more than twenty years. But in Syracuse I found that there was a non-artistic, business side to this position that I was just starting to understand.

A ballet director, I learned, is frequently called upon to be very involved in the finances, the budget matters, and the fund raising aspects of the company. Most of the time, this isn't why ballet dancers accept the role of director, and I was both unfamiliar with it and not particularly interested in the business side at the time. Moreover, the Board had instructed me to mount a *Nutcracker* production. Promises were made and assurances given by the Board members that they would raise the funds needed for this production, but these pledges evaporated as the time grew nearer. I felt utterly alone at this point. The same people who hired me and encouraged me to do major works were suddenly unwilling to fulfill their roles and were becoming adversarial. The constant petty bickering seemed unnecessary and counterproductive. I longed for Gloria and some harmony.

We began to discuss marriage in the spring or summer of June, 1978, and I was growing impatient. The winter in upstate New York was brutal and lonely. My heart was in the artistic activities but not the political battling and lack of support. I finally gave the Board members a firm statement about the funds needed for the *Nutcracker*, and explained that I would resign unless they fulfilled their promises. They didn't, and I kept my word. At the time, I was singed a bit. It was very disappointing to have my first major role as an artistic director turn out so dismally. Yet I knew my departure was hastened by my wanting to be with Gloria. The idea dawned on me that for once, my heart, not my career, was leading me.

Though disappointed by this experience, I wasn't devastated by it. I attribute this to my strong spirituality, knowing that events happen for a reason, though we don't always comprehend it at the time. It was God's plan; one had to trust and have faith. This experience was supposed to have this outcome, and Mr. Balanchine and I agreed that it was already known in the spiritual world. "Be more spiritual in dealing with life's occurrences," he'd gently remind me in my earlier years with the City Ballet. I kept picturing Balanchine's own words describing two strangers about to meet on a corner, a meeting that might change their lives, yet minutes before they are oblivious to it. Yes, I learned my craft from Mr. Balanchine, but I think the philosophical and spiritual principles were perhaps more powerful. Spiritual guidance also came in the form of the

Reverend Marge LaJudas, the spiritual leader of the Church of Universal Brotherhood in New York. Having family members with psychic knowledge, I recognized that she too could see into the future. She suggested that I start a school on Long Island in 1979. Although Mr. Balanchine and Marge La Judas never met one another, they were both crucial in convincing me to come to Long Island to start a school.

Back in the other world, *Vienna Waltzes* came into being. In February of 1977 Mr. Balanchine started choreographing this beautiful ballet. He told me that the Board had always wanted him to produce a ballet for the box office. One morning, in the midst of choreographing this new work, Mr. Balanchine came to teach class, and scanned the room, all the faces, finally pointing to me and three others, saying "You will be teachers." I was supremely complimented. Mr. Balanchine did not compliment anyone often. He never showered us with praise. To have received a compliment of this magnitude from my own master teacher was a cherished moment I relive again and again.

Mr. Balanchine wanted me to learn the lead in the first movement of *Vienna Waltzes* understudying Jacques d'Amboise, and I did. When Jacques was injured, though, another dancer, Sean Lavery substituted for him, and partnered Karin von Aroldingen. It was right.

I had had my time. Sean was tall and a fine partner for Karin and it is important if not vital to continually develop new talent in a company. The philosophical or spiritual approach had indeed enabled me to see this as the way it should be.

GEORGE BALANCHINE, FRANK OHMAN, JUDY FUGATE
REHEARSING VIENNA WALTZES, 1977

I was amused when I thought of how I would have reacted years earlier when I was an untamed cowboy, new to the company. I would have been angry and upset, perhaps even unprofessional or reckless. I was different now. To teach Balanchine's legacy to generations of children was what I was supposed to do next, not fret over a role. Thus, instead of partnering Karin in *Vienna Waltzes*, I was in the finale, dancing the waltz to Strauss's *Der Rosenkavalier* and I partnered Judy Fugate, a wonderful waltzer. It is a wonderfully romantic and deservedly popular ballet.

I thought it wise to take a break from all outside professional activities, like choreographing and touring with New York Dance Theater, during the first year of my marriage. Gloria and I were married in her church in Maryland in June 1978. For that year, I danced only with the New York City Ballet. I think Mr. Balanchine was a little nervous about me. He knew well my history of relationships. He said, "Frank, continue dancing as long as you can."

He was also quietly helping me, knowing that keeping me in *Union Jack* and *Vienna Waltzes* and other repertory pieces gave me the salary I needed to start my school. Mr. Balanchine and I conversed regularly about the process of starting one. Mr. B knew I wanted a school to train my own students to dance in the Balanchine style, and also become a base for the New York Dance

Theater. He told me, "Frank, you must educate the parents. There are so many well-intentioned parents who don't understand or investigate ballet schools. They don't know the importance of good classical training or don't check the credentials of the school's director or teachers."

He had identified the problem so precisely and accurately. I was to learn for years thereafter that caring parents looked at geographic proximity, time, and cost, without examining the level and quality of the ballet training, or even inquiring about the credentials of the staff. Equality does not reign in the land of American ballet schools.

In the late seventies, I was continuing to dance with the company though I knew I was past my prime. I think a mature dancer can infuse certain roles with a maturity, a conservation of movement that incorporates all that he has learned in his career. Mostly I stayed because I wanted to be with Mr. Balanchine for as long as I could, and I think he wanted that too. He was my reason for remaining.

At this time, the spectacular Misha Baryshnikov joined the City Ballet. His presence alone at the New York City Ballet was electrifying. At a matinee performance, he premiered in *Coppelia*. What an incredible dancer! The acclaim he has garnered over the years is deserved. Initially, when he joined the City Ballet, he was learning roles, and seemed very quiet. The time wasn't ideal for him to join the company. Mr. Balanchine, uncharacteristically, wasn't around that much to help him. He was having a cataract operation. Though a huge and gifted star, the roles Baryshnikov was dancing were not made to exploit his particular gifts. Misha certainly made an easy transition into the City Ballet family. There was no friction; he regularly took company class. We spoke a few times. He was friendly, and I know we would have been closer had I not been spending all my free time with Gloria in Maryland, so I wasn't around much. I never did get to learn from Misha the trick to doing a double *tour jete* landing in *arabesque*. I just never had the opportunity to ask him the secret.

At the close of the decade of the seventies, the City Ballet prepared to go to London on tour. Gloria was coming with me, and I was delighted. She had never been to Europe and we could be together. She still had her Maryland school and company, and her elderly parents, so we were still commuting, as we did when we were dating. A commuter marriage is very difficult, and is so especially in the early months of a marriage.

Before leaving for the tour, Susie Hendl called me and related that Mr. Balanchine wanted me to learn and perform *Le Bourgeois Gentilhomme*. I was delighted, as always. The company met at Kennedy Airport for the London flight. Mr. Balanchine was cute, and a bit coy when I brought Gloria in to meet him in London's Covent Garden. I introduced them. Mr. Balanchine said, "You have a new raincoat, Frank." I answered, "It's a London Fog...and I bought it in Macy's in New York." He was amused. He seemed to be happy that I was married, but little expressions, words and pauses made me think he wasn't sure how it would work out. When we were alone for a moment, he reiterated, "Don't quit the company."

Away from everyone and together finally, Gloria and I had fun in England. We rode double-decker buses, and visited fine museums. Since I had only *Union Jack* and rehearsals for *Le Bourgeois Gentilhomme,* Gloria and I went to Edinburgh, Scotland for a weekend. Though we headed there by rail, we walked all over Edinburgh, enjoying the castles like two kids.

I rehearsed for *Gentilhomme* with Susie Hendl and Ib Anderson, who was learning Peter Martins' role. It was exciting, and right after each rehearsal, I phoned Gloria at our hotel, filling her in on all the details. As dancers, we spoke the same shorthand language. Mr. Balanchine had set this piece years earlier for the Ballet Russe de Monte Carlo and then for City Opera.

My trip was wonderful in these respects but sad in others. Though I didn't want to fully acknowledge it, I knew this would probably be my final tour with the New York City Ballet. How would I ever be able to depart from this company?

Back in New York, I thought my eventual departure might be easier if I took the first steps to starting a school on Long Island. I resolved to act, and not just plan. Just after taking photographs in my *La Valse* costume for the new City Ballet program, I took the train to Long Island where my friend Susan Pimsluer met me in the Syosset train station. We drove over to several possible locations. My school has humble but solid beginnings.

I decided to begin my school by holding classes in the basement of the Methodist Church in Centerport. Later, I moved it to a flat above a Chinese restaurant in Greenlawn. It would take two more moves until I would put down roots in June 1990 in Commack, Long Island. But my first place, the Church basement, became my starting point. All winter I commuted from New York City to Long Island. In the beginning, I had a record player and a record from Melissa Hayden, no *barre* but a post that held up the floor of the church.

Unfortunately, Gloria returned to Maryland, to her family, and her school. Her father had been ill, and she was concerned, wanting to be in closer proximity. My mother thought my relationship with Gloria was very strange. She told me that a couple should at least live in the same state or city; she didn't believe in this commuter-type relationship.

Those first few months of the school were trying,

as it always is when one begins something brand new. I knew little about business, and operating a school requires business savvy. I trusted Board members to see to this aspect of the school's operation, and it was a mistake. I was naïve, too, and some Board members were without scruples. There were setbacks with co-workers. My choreographic efforts had been put aside temporarily while trying to establish a school, and I missed having this creative outlet. It wasn't only the school that troubled me. My wife was in another state and I knew it wouldn't be long before I had to say goodbye to my other family, the City Ballet.

Shortly thereafter, I moved to the room over the Chinese restaurant in Greenlawn for my school. I slept in the studio overnight in a sleeping bag as I had early Saturday morning classes. The Chinese restaurant had great food, and I eat there still. The restaurant owners were always complaining, though, about the jumping. I guess many people would have thought this situation odd, a soloist from the New York City Ballet sleeping on the floor, but I was raised to work hard and be humble. Indeed, floors are good to sleep on, at least for this dancer's back. A good meal was just one flight away, too. Mostly, I was driven to continue the Balanchine dance tradition by training generations of young dancers. I wanted to pass on his legacy.

By the summer of 1980 I was devoting my full

time to the school and dancing only occasionally in New York City Ballet roles. I invited ballerina Melissa Hayden to come out to my school on Long Island and set Mr. Balanchine's *Pas de Dix* in the spring of 1982. Though we had started off on such horrendous footing so many years ago, it was short-lived and Melissa rapidly became one of my fondest friends and a wonderful, astute advisor.

As she had before, on this trip she made a wise suggestion. "Why don't you do a *Nutcracker*?" she asked. I had to think it over. It was a tremendous undertaking, I knew, and required lots of scenery and costumes as well. I decided it was worth undertaking, and it would be a version after Balanchine's own. Happily, it is now a regular holiday institution on Long Island, and an annual success.

In June of 1982, Mr. Balanchine was staging *Noah and the Flood* to Stravinsky's score. Richard Dryden called me and said, "Mr. Balanchine would like you to be in it, Frank. Would you come to the State Theater and be the one to hold the tree of life?" I would have said yes to anything Mr. B wanted me to do, of course, but this seemed to be imbued with significance. It is easy to weave or impose one's own interpretation on the acts of others, perhaps inflating one's own self-importance. I continually check myself in this area, to be certain I am not venturing into the realm of fantastic wish fulfillment. But this request of Mr. Balanchine's, the role itself, and his behavior did leave me believing it had a larger, symbolic significance.

When I arrived at Lincoln Center, I saw that the whole company was rehearsing this piece at the New York State Theater; it was our entire City Ballet family. The actor John Houseman was there as well, as the piece's narrator, and so was Robert Irving, our conductor. The main hall was filled. "Mr. B hired me almost twenty years ago to the day," I suddenly realized. I stood holding the tree of life, which I was honored to do, and I began sensing some symbolic responsibility, even a foreshadowing of some kind. Dressed all in black, I shook the tree for Adam and Eve. Mr. Balanchine came in through the same side door, near the elevators, which he had always used on the fifth level of the State Theater. He scanned the faces, walked across the rehearsal floor, bypassing everyone else and came directly to me. He shook my hand, and asked how I was. I was so happy to see him, so honored that he came to greet me personally, so esteemed that he had chosen me for this role. I would have done any role or even job, for that matter, he asked of me, from mopping the floor to packing costumes. It didn't matter.

We were once again to perform in our summer home of Saratoga in upstate New York in 1982, but an uneasiness, an anxiety was gripping the company. Mr. Balanchine was not at the theater in Saratoga. Mr. B was always ubiquitous in whatever theater we were to use, so this was strange and unsettling. Something was terribly wrong.

The company traveled to Washington D.C.'s Kennedy Center after performing in Saratoga; it was there that Barbara Horgan announced that Mr. Balanchine was in the hospital. We were all silent and stunned, like a group of young children suddenly realizing the absence of a parent. It seemed Mr. Balanchine, who was a father figure, role model, and friend to so many of us, was suffering from a neurological disorder.

His symptoms included a loss of balance and dizzy spells. I sped over to the hospital to visit him, and there he was, sleeping peacefully. Not wanting to disturb him, I just prayed this was a temporary ailment and he would soon recover. This was not to be.

Once the company returned to New York, Mr. Balanchine entered nearby Roosevelt Hospital. What an enormous strain this must have been for him. He was ill, but he still was scheduling seasons, restaging, casting, and managing the myriad of day to day matters that are inherent in running a major company. He had always managed everything, from checking on the costumes, to teaching company class each morning, to overseeing the School of American Ballet, to watching the company every night from downstage right wing of the theater. For us dancers, his absence didn't create an extra burden in terms of work but rather left us adrift, untethered. There had never been anyone else, you see, as our leader. Mr. Balanchine had overseen all aspects of the company, and amazingly had still found time to make a lasting personal impression on each one of us.

Mr. Balanchine remained in Roosevelt Hospital for about six months. I visited him regularly. I kept praying and picturing him getting up out of bed, and walking out of the hospital. Time and again I imagined him walking into class as always, sleeves rolled up, wearing his cowboy shirt and tie, making a joke, or having fun interacting with the dancers while choreographing his next new work. I pictured him in his intensely quiet way during one of our private talks, listening so closely yet so respectful in his comments and gingerly offering me advice. I thought of the man I had met so long ago, who had changed my life. He was responsible for giving me a glorious career with a stellar company, but more importantly, he taught me to want to be a better person, in every way.

His spiritual or philosophical gift to me was that we are each here for reasons known to God. As individuals we must discover our own personal mission, our reason for being here, and then fulfill it. Our life's journey is to find the answer to the question, "why am I here?" Thereafter, one should pursue one's life work as honestly, devotedly, and kindly as one can. My grandmother and my mother had shaped and cultivated my life philosophy and goals, and Mr. Balanchine had enriched, extended it, and taught me to carry out my life's work in the context of contributing something to the world, to humanity.

I was realizing his many gifts to me during his hospital stay. One gift was this philosophical or spiritual view of life and our role in this world; another gift box was overflowing with fatherly concern and support throughout the highs and lows of my personal life. Yet another present was learning how to have respectful and meaningful relationships with women. Three more boxes contained the gifts of how to teach, choreograph, and dance.

Mr. Balanchine had also bestowed on me the gift of understanding what it means to be a true artist. I had read about and watched artists all my life, in person, in books, on stage and screen. I had learned dance technique and perfected my talents. But this isn't what makes someone an artist. To be a great artist one must care deeply and completely about something, and to work devotedly to contribute that artistry to the world. The goal is never widespread acclaim or financial rewards. Mr. Balanchine was one of the greatest artists the world has ever known. He was a gift to us all.

I visited him regularly in the hospital. During one visit, when his dizziness was particularly acute, Mr. Balanchine said, "When I get out of the hospital, I probably won't be able to choreograph. I'll have to learn a different profession." We both laughed at that. Though ill, he could still be so humorous. Mr. Balanchine asked me about my school, and I told him about it. He said he'd come out and visit it when he was better. Another time, I walked into his hospital room and there he was watching wrestling on television. "Look," he said with that twinkle in his eye, "choreography."

When winter came, and it was snowing, I once entered his room while a School of American Ballet faculty member, Andre Kramarevsky was visiting too. Mr. Balanchine looked at me and said, "If you are going to stay, you must do turns for me." So there, in the antiseptic white environment of the hospital room, with only the clanking of the wheels on hospital carts to accompany me, I did turns, wearing my clunky winter boots. "OK," Mr. Balanchine said, jovially, "You can stay." I called him New Year's Eve to wish him a happy one, and we spoke briefly.

On a later visit, he offered me some chocolates which he had received as a gift. There we sat, both of us, on the hospital bed, side by side, he in his hospital gown and me in my streeclothes munching on chocolates, contentedly and comfortably quiet. He was in a fine mood that day, though he had never let on if he was uncomfortable or in pain or sad. In Russian, he recited a poem for me, and then told me, "Sixty-five years ago, I learned that." I couldn't begin to tell him how much I had learned from him, but I knew I could express how much he meant to me. I told Mr. Balanchine I loved him. He understood. It was the last of our private talks.

I have never forgotten the circumstances the surroundings, the time, and the people when I have received dreadful news. The scene is branded into my memory. Time stops; my thoughts are halted; I am immobilized. So it was when I walked into my ballet school that Saturday morning, April 30, 1983, when one of my board members, sitting at the desk with her head bowed, lifted her head with its solemn expression, and said, "Frank, did you hear? Mr. Balanchine passed away." I had sudden stomach pains as if I had just received a powerful blow. I felt winded and couldn't speak. I couldn't seem to get air into my lungs. The board member continued sympathetically, "We have arranged for another teacher to take your class for today." Her comment brought me back to earth. I knew what I had to do. With utmost conviction and with a strength that surprised me, I replied firmly, "No. I am going to teach. I'm doing what he told me I would be doing, and what he wanted me to do." And though it was emotionally so painful a day, I knew I was doing the right thing. Mr. Balanchine had shown me that.

I called my Mom that day to tell her the devastating news. She had already heard about Mr. Balanchine's passing. I went to visit her, to gain strength. I felt completely lost.

I was numb during Mr. Balanchine's funeral, so I can recall just fleeting, sensory, scenes from that awful day. Bob Maiorano and I met at the State Theater, looked at each other's profoundly sad faces, and understood each other's intense grief. My only words to my friend were, "We are on our own now."

The funeral service was held at a Russian Orthodox Church in New York City. I do remember that it was a full service, and I recall that all the company members, his children, sat up front, near his open casket. Rosemary Dunleavy came up to me and threw her arms around me; we were one in grief. Lincoln solemnly said to me, "There's a great void now." At one point I remember standing for several hours, holding a white lit candle, as did others. George Balanchine was buried along with Danilova in Sag Harbor, on Long Island. I try to go every summer to visit them. Once I sat there in my car and had *Serenade* by Tchaikovsky playing on my car radio. I take some solace in knowing his final resting place is not far from me.

Chapter Eight: Coming Full Circle

"Most ballet teachers in the US are terrible. If they
were in medicine, everyone would be poisoned."
GEORGE BALANCHINE

I had a dream recently that I was walking down Broadway towards Lincoln Center, and there I spotted Mr. Balanchine, walking across the street, obviously trying not to have eye contact with me, which means he was planning some surprise. Even now, years after his death, Mr. Balanchine is in my heart, my thoughts, and my dreams. So many years later, I am still so often moved to tears by the memory of him.

One year after Mr. Balanchine's death, I officially left the New York City Ballet. What was the point in staying on? I had stayed to be with him and my reason for staying was now gone.

My last actual performance was in July of 1983 in Saratoga. I was the comical Burgomaster in *Coppelia*. Examining the contents of my theater case at that final moment of my dancing career would have revealed some tights, weights, a robe, biographies, character shoes, makeup. Unremarkable, I suppose. But what is noteworthy is that I never took it with me nor did I ever go to collect it. My theater case was shipped, along with those of all the other company members, from Saratoga to the New York State Theater at Lincoln Center, and I never retrieved it. This somehow made my parting less formal, perhaps less final. Even with Mr. Balanchine gone, it was so terribly hard to face leaving the company. Though it has no doubt long since been discarded, I like to imagine that my theater bag is there at the New York State Theater, with the company that I have never completely left and which has never really left me.

My mother was terribly upset at Mr. Balanchine's death. She was deeply affected for some time. Shortly after his death, she dreamt of Mr. Balanchine, and in her dream, he told her, "I'm not dead; I'm just resting." We were both soothed by the words he uttered in her dream. Knowing his prescient nature, he was probably right, as always.

I moved my mother in to live with me as she grew older and was falling frequently in her own apartment. I took care of her for two and a half years until it was clear she needed full-time care. I am grateful for this time as it gave us the opportunity to become closer, which was wonderful. One of our favorite activities was taking long drives to the beach, where we would relax and talk about the significant and the insignificant. I rediscovered after so many years that she really knew what was right and what was wrong. Finally, after her health deteriorated greatly and she had to enter a nursing home, where she lived for two years, my brave, wise, and loving mother died in June 1989. She too is buried on Long Island, within a few miles of my home. The losses of my mother and Mr. Balanchine have left the greatest voids in my life. Yet their spirits and their beliefs are always with me.

Gloria did not like Long Island and returned to Maryland. My mother, who had predicted very rough marital terrain with two people living in different states, was again right. My marriage did not last, but Gloria and I do have a beautiful son, Johan, who has graduated from college and graduate school. He provides financial advice to non-profit organizations and small businesses. My mother was thrilled that at age eighty-one, she finally became a grandmother. His birth was one of the most ecstatic and momentous periods of my life. I felt a tidal wave of joy as this tiny infant scrutinized me and tugged at my hair with miniature yet perfect pink fingers. I felt love wash over and through me from the moment I saw his tiny face in the hospital nursery. I still feel that way today, whether I am watching him study, play the trumpet, or play baseball.

FRANK WITH SON JOHAN, AGE TWO

Since leaving the New York City Ballet, I have spent much of my time being a pioneer of sorts on Long Island. I guess that means I am back to being a cowboy again. As my master teacher, Mr. B, so astutely advised, it is a rigorous mission to educate well-intentioned but not well-informed parents about the importance of proper classical ballet training. I have had so many students transfer to my school after spending years elsewhere and sadly reveal that they learned more in one week in my school than they did in all their years in another school. Numerous times, parents have recognized the difference in training when their children are much older, and have told me, "All those years wasted." This is not to promote myself as the only qualified teacher; rather, it is to create awareness in families to investigate a ballet school's instructors, their training, and their philosophy.

I have taken to calling schools that emphasize only the end of the year recital, and do not try to give students a thorough and solid ballet background, fast-food dancing schools. Solid classical training enabled me to reach the heights of the world of dance that would not have occurred if I had been instructed and drilled only in selected elements for a year-end show. It saddens me when I see this happen again and again to children who truly love dancing. Interestingly, I have learned that in Europe they don't have a tremendous number of fast food dance schools. The recital-only mentality takes a while to change but I feel I have made inroads on Long Island and I continuously work to alter families' awareness about the differences.

As a pioneer/teacher, I also try to protect students against injury. It is so important to have proper dance training that prevents injury as much as possible. I also check my students' legs for tightness, and some are advised to perhaps stretch more, or do some strength or flexibility-building exercises. One of my students attended a special out-of-state college program recently. She called to tell me that half of the class was injured, and added, "You really trained us properly." Another former student wrote me, "I cannot count the number of young girls I have come to know who have "studied" dance at various schools, who complain of pain, injury, shin splints, neck and back problems, and who after all their "training," still had bad posture!"

This is part of my drive, my mission, which my mother and grandmother and Mr. Balanchine helped me shape and refine. My role in this stage of my post-dancing life is to continue to train new generations of children in the Balanchine style of classical ballet, and to choreograph new works in traditional and other media. Naturally I incorporate his techniques in my school. I teach Mr. Balanchine's *tendu battement,* for instance, which is different than others. With Mr. B's technique, the leg does not go out with the pointed toe leading; instead, the leg moves directly forward with the foot, from heel to toe, kept straight, and horizontal, not angled. My students, too, are accustomed to having a ball in their palms to learn the correct positions of the hands and fingers.

I use everyday observations, like my mentor, to give students a visual image of what we are striving for, such as telling the students to "land softly like a pussycat...not like Puss in Boots." My students have heard me tell them to rotate their hands "like a flower opening," as Mr. B would instruct us.

Moreover, I personalize my instruction, as Mr. Balanchine did. The class is a group of individuals, of people whom I am teaching, not a faceless or uniform group of dance students. Thus, I don't rehearse the same steps the same way with different students. I correct the individual's movement, not the class's movement. I view each student as a person and as a dancer as I walk around the studio making individual corrections. My students sense this. Several have told me, "I feel you are seeing me." Another said, "I feel you are paying attention to me. Other teachers teach ballet but you see me, and talk to me."

I try to use humor as Mr. Balanchine did; it relaxes the children just as it relaxed me in Mr. B's class decades ago. As I observed with my master teacher, I try to put aside personal worries and concerns when I step into the classroom. I focus and concentrate completely, trying to be with them, in the present moment. My dancing career was excellent training for this. When I was performing four ballets a night, I didn't worry about the third ballet; I concentrated only on my first ballet, and when it concluded, I turned my full attention to ballet number two, and so forth.

I strive to become as fine a teacher as I can be. Teaching the art that has been my life is a great pleasure, and I want to pass on as much as possible to younger generations. Keeping Mr. Balanchine's life and legacy alive is not my only goal, though. As he taught me, we can't live in the past. But I do work to incorporate his philosophy about life in my own and in my work, and to perhaps expand on it. When I teach, I am not just teaching steps or movement, but a legacy of great art. As my master teacher taught us to have the larger, respectful perspective on what we were learning, I try to do the same. I communicate the importance of what the students are doing. They should understand they are part of a great tradition. Hence my students have heard of all the great composers, the great choreographers, and major figures, like Lincoln Kirstein. One student wrote me, "Thank you for teaching me ballet and for teaching me to love ballet." I have been privileged to be part of a great tradition, and I hope I can be one link, however small, in this continuous chain of this art, bringing young people to into this chain, too.

Teaching is rather noble, I feel. Perhaps I am making a contribution in guiding children to art and beauty and hopefully away from drugs and violence. I like to have the opportunity to be a positive force in the lives of children, to guide them, to help them learn, to give them someone to talk to. I like to think I teach young people the art of ballet but I hope I also teach young people through the art of ballet.

Parents often ask me for advice. What would I recommend their children do to enhance their abilities as dancers? A student, I've come to learn, needs to be influenced by good classical movement, watch good classical performances and attend classes. To learn, a student must be humble and open to being corrected. But the character of the person his or her willingness to work hard, to be dedicated, to try, to be sincere is as important as her dancing abilities.

Mr. Balanchine, my master teacher, made me want to be a better person. He exemplified the traits he valued: dedication, loyalty, hard work, and honesty. I try to pass that lesson on to my students by being a role model myself. I am honest with my students, and I give them sincere feedback. If a student has problems with her feet, to use a simple example, I inform her, and instruct her how to work on it. I reinforce the right things, like working hard, not necessarily doing the highest turns. I try to be fair in my casting, particularly when it comes to coveted roles in my Nutcracker. I try to reward loyalty too; I don't care for those demanding yet lazy, nomadic students who leave my school if they don't get a major *Nutcracker* role, attend other schools, and then want to return, as inappropriately self-promoting as ever.

I have been blessed in my life. Though the world has become so cynical, the simple values I was taught really brought about my success and happiness. My school has a wonderful reputation and my name as a dancer and choreographer in New York has become better known. My career has been steady and I have always been privileged to remain in my chosen profession.

I have been so blessed to have the help of my City Ballet colleagues in making the school successful. Many dancers, including Peter Martins, Ben Huys, Stacy Caddell, Bob Maiorano, Peter Boal, Helene Alexopoulos, Teresa Reyes, Miriam Mahdaviani, Peter Frame, Nicole Hlinka, Robert La Fosse, Lindsay Fischer, Lauren Hauser, and Kipling Houston have performed in my Nutcracker or given master classes. Merrill Ashley came out in 1989 to do a gala for me. What a wonderful dancer and a long-time friend. Their help and support have been invaluable and they continue to help out all the time.

I don't know where I would have been without the parents of my dance students when my school moved from Huntington to Commack. They helped me lay the floors and construct the partitions; we all carried lumber and became a construction crew. The Thompsons, Howard and Joan, whose daughter Susie had been my student since the age of six, were especially my Long Island angels, helping me and seeing me through some very tough challenges. I guess my early career building our home with my step-father Eddie was excellent training. Susie, who also danced with my chamber group, wrote me recently, "Learning from you as a student and then working with you as a member of your company...I was in the presence of greatness, a great person and a great artist."

Mostly I think I was a guy who wanted to dance. With hard work, with humility, with faith, I learned with and from the best, and saw my childhood dreams come true.

My master teachers taught me that the most important elements in life are not necessarily that which we can see. Mr. Balanchine succeeded in making ballet its own distinct recognizable art form and he created a classical yet modern dance form. His gifts to me included the drive to be a better person and the lifelong goal of fulfilling one's potential. And several of the parents whose sons and daughters have been my students have written me notes with the greatest of compliments: "You have the spirit of Balanchine." I don't know if that is true or not, but I do feel his spirit with me.

Not long ago, I was choreographing a major work and was near completion. Yet something amorphous was nagging at me. Something was missing from the work, I decided. I pondered yet couldn't determine what the ballet was lacking. I drove out to Mr. B's former Long Island house, and parked in front of it, thinking for a time. The very next day, I knew what was missing, what was necessary to add. The scene and the steps flowed easily then.

For years, as a New York City Ballet dancer, I stood in the same spot at the *barre*, in front of the door, in Mr. B's classes. Not long ago, I returned to the same studio but this time with one of my wonderful students, Susie Thompson. I brought Susie into the same studio, though now I was the teacher and she the student. I asked her to warm up, because she was Sugar Plum Fairy in my *Nutcracker*, and she had to rehearse. Without a word from me, Susie went to my exact spot at the *barre*. The room was huge and empty, but she chose that spot. To see the circle, the continuation of life and legacy is gratifying indeed.

I had a particularly gifted student, Sabrina, who is now a young adult. She studied with me since the age of six. The role of the Sugar Plum Fairy in *The Nutcracker* is a coveted one, and is sought after in my annual production. Parents begin promoting their children in the fall; speculation and rumors abound, and even when cast, competitive counting begins to see which dancer does more "Sugar Plums" than another. I have actively discouraged this but it persists, unfortunately. I stopped off in Sabrina's neighborhood one day to ask her to do three performances as "Sugar Plum." There she was, running a lawn mower in her front yard. No prima donna she; Sabrina accepted her ordinary chores without hesitation. She turned off the motor when she saw me and came to greet me.

"Sabrina," I asked, "would you like to do three performances as "Sugar Plum?" She smiled. "Two is fine, Mr. Ohman," she said. Sabrina was sensational in the role. Another dancer, though, had bungled her performance in the role of "Sugar Plum" and desperately wanted another chance.

Without encouragement or a sign from anyone, Sabrina voluntarily gave her one of her solo performances. Character is inseparable from the dancer, after all, and besides that which we see technique, precision, artistry, musicality there are the qualities we can't see humility, dedication, kindness, loyalty but are perhaps even more important. Standing in the wings, I nodded, deeply gratified, when I watched Sabrina's self-chosen replacement dance, and I got the sense that others whom I knew so well, though not necessarily visible, were smiling too.

Post Script

*"Have great patience and make students trust
themselves that they can do it."*
FRANK OHMAN

S ince the late 1990s, I've continued to teach
Mr. Balanchine's legacy in my school, now
entering its thirty-fourth year, as well
as share it nationally and internationally. His
wisdom about life still informs everything I do,
and I try to pass it along to future generations.

In honor of the 100th anniversary of Mr.
Balanchine's birth, in 2004, I thought it a fitting
tribute to offer public lectures and demonstrations.
We offered presentations in libraries across
Long Island and one library in Connecticut
with my advanced ballet students. My students
performed variations from *Agon, Stars and Stripes*,
and the "Fascinatin' Rhythm" section of *Who
Cares*. How wonderful to see people of all ages
attend, absorb, and enjoy the ground-breaking,
classic, and still thrilling works of this genius. As

I have periodically since Mr. B's passing, I felt his presence at our Connecticut presentation.

I had the immense good fortune to share Balanchine's ballet techniques and training with Ballet Philippines. Thanks to their generosity, I was a Master Artist in Residence for one month in April, 2004. How gratifying to teach classes each day, with the very fine dancers of the company, about twenty-five ballerinas and about fifteen male dancers. I was so impressed with their focus and desire to learn. They were a classical ballet company that incorporated their own style and performed their own, wonderful choreography. I observed that the Philippine people, in general, seemed enthralled with the arts. Interestingly, the male dancers did not appear to face the same stereotypes or embarrassment that I did at their age. I'm glad they didn't have to pretend their ballet bag was a bowling bag as I did!

Still, their training was quite different from the Balanchine tradition. The ballerinas, for instance, came to class with their shins bandaged. They were in pain, but why? I began to play detective and realized the cause: the floor. Classes and rehearsals were held on a hard floor, comprised of only planks. To prevent injuries, a spring floor would be much better. I made up plans for a Mr. B-type lattice-spring floor, and instructed the carpenters to build it in sections, so it could easily be disassembled and reassembled; in other words, the floor was portable and could even be moved to the stage. The floors were finished just after I completed my time with the Company, but they were incredibly grateful and told me the new floors helped immensely.

I found the male dancers of the Company very strong, but after my first class, they returned the following day with sore muscles, due to the emphasis on turnout in my class.

I'm not sure the dancers had ever waltzed before, but they were so eager to learn, that I taught them a different waltz daily.

On weekends the Company director, some dancers, and I traveled about 200 miles by dirt road to Batangas, a popular visitor destination known for its beaches. How beautiful it was. I slept outside the boathouse so I could walk along the beach which was gorgeous at night. "What a perfect place for painting," I thought, and hope someday to return and do just that.

It is so gratifying to see new audiences and generations introduced to Balanchine's work. In 2005, New York City Ballet principal ballerina, Suzanne Farrell, now the head of her own dance company, invited all the dancers in the original cast of Mr. B's *Don Quixote* to her premiere restaging of the same ballet. Held in the majestic Kennedy Center in Washington, D.C., I reunited with my New York City Ballet colleagues and friends, including Kay Mazzo, Carol Sumner, and Mimi Paul. At a gorgeous gala the night before the ballet, Suzanne approached me and said, "His presence...he's here." I knew exactly who and what she meant. I was experiencing it, too. "Yes, I know, Suzanne," I answered.

Even though I had been cast and danced in all three acts of *Don Quixote*, I had never seen it from the audience's vantage point; this is a common occurrence for ballet dancers. So it was a wonderful experience, seeing it this way. The music had a wonderful mood to it, so very different than the original, Russian version. I realized the ballet had premiered in 1965, and here it was 2005, forty years later. Kay Mazzo, a superb New York City Ballet dancer, was sitting just behind me. I looked back at her and said, "You remember every note, right?" "Yes!" she exclaimed. Once a dancer, always a dancer. How wonderful Suzanne was in this ballet, and how brilliantly she taught her dancers.

My school has grown and progressed in wonderful ways. In 2008-09 we moved to new, larger, brighter facilities in Commack, NY. Our new school was an incredible gift; I am so fortunate that my reputation led to this facility literally being reconstructed for me. New wood floors without hard or metal components were built. Each member of the construction crew was given one of my watercolors as a gift. The reopening of the new ballet school brought alumni, former students, friends, even government leaders to the event. All the values I had been taught throughout my life — hard work, dedication, character, humility — had once again brought me invaluable rewards.

I was rewarded again, personally, when my son, Johan, came to live with me on Long Island for about two years. I had, of course, been visiting him regularly for years, especially during Christmas holidays and summer vacations, but this was a blessing. I immediately noticed the fine job my ex-wife Gloria had done as a parent; she raised him to love and respect me. I observed that we had so many similar character traits: Johan rose early daily, commuted to New York City, and never missed a day of work. He too loves Bach, though I told him that when he's older, he'll love Brahms, like his father. In fact, I had a show at Hofstra University in the summer of 2012. I choreographed a special piece for Johan, set to Bach's *Piano concerto in D Minor*. He adored it.

In 2009 my school's board said they would like to have an Annual Gala and asked who I thought should be invited to be honored. I thought for about fifteen seconds and said Jacques d'Amboise, who became our first honoree in 2010. When I joined the company in 1962 he was well known to me as I had seen him in *Carousel* and *Seven Brides for Seven Brothers*, one of my favorite films of all time. Jacques helped me a great deal and was a good friend to me. My school has been part of Jacques's National Dance Institute working with the hearing impaired.

Allegra Kent was our 2011 honoree. I danced with Allegra in *Agon* and *Allegro Brilliante* at the New York City Ballet. She also taught me the *Apollo* pas de deux, and we performed it in concert. Both Allegra and Jacques taught master classes for me when I first started my school, and have attended all of our events.

In 2012 we honored Arthur Mitchell. When I first joined the company, Arthur was a constant source of encouragement. Edward Villella was our 2013 honoree. He was an astounding, brilliantly gifted dancer who went on to create a first-rate company in Miami. Despite his incredible accomplishments, he is still a man of humility. We were thrilled when Eddie, a native New Yorker, decided to return home! I danced with Eddie's touring group quite a bit.

All of these wonderful dancers were part of the company when I joined City Ballet in July of 1962, and we were all on that initial trip to the Soviet Union.

I so wish that Millie Hayden was still with us so that we could honor her. She was my friend and I loved her.

After a lifetime of dancing, teaching, and mentoring, some might think that I'm eager for retirement. I have no such plan. My life has been as an artist, a ballet dancer, and now teaching ballet to generation after generation, particularly the Balanchine tradition. I'm filled with joy and gratitude that I've realized my dream with the incalculable support of my grandmother, my mother, my wonderful colleagues, teachers, and Mr. Balanchine. I never had connections or resources, but with diligent study, devotion, and a bit of luck, I became what I had dreamt of. I hope to inspire young talented people, in any field, to strive for the same. You can do it.

FRANK OHMAN - BALLET MASTER

ACKNOWLEDGEMENTS

I'd like to thank the wonderful individuals who served so loyally on my Board of Directors from 1986 to the present. In alphabetical order, they are: Mr. and Mrs. Arragon, Mrs. Joanne Arroya, Mrs. Sharon Barth. MaryEllen Bruno, Andrea Cillo, Michelle Dalpiaz, Mr. and Mrs. Richard DiAndrea, Ms. Kathi DiAndrea, Erin and Joseph Drennan, Maria Fohsz, Kathy Kairnes, Maureen and Gene Koch, Darrell, Diane, and Danielle Lichtenberger, Mrs. Argere Loizides, Ms. Lauren Loschiavo, Laurence and Julie Lycksell, Gino and Vasi Malatesta, Laura Matturro, Mrs. Cora McGerald, Johan Ohman, Helen Papa, Glenn Peterson, Mrs. Barbara Rossi, Mr. and Mrs. Michael Shef, John and Sylvia Simeone, Mr. and Mrs. William Simpson, Ms. Lynne Stuccio, Howard and Joan Thompson.

I am grateful to my trusted Advisory Panel, who include: Emily Berkowitz, Mark Peterson, Francis Sackett and Paul Sackett.

To my loyal ballet mistresses, my anchors, Diane Lichtenberger and Donna Floridia, my heartfelt gratitude.

I am also indebted, and forever grateful, to so many New York City Ballet colleagues and other dancers for dancing, teaching and providing assistance at my school. They include: Helene Alexopoulos, Merrill Ashley, Peter Boal, Bonita Borne, Leslie Browne, Stacy Caddell, Jacques d'Amboise, Gerald Ebitz, Lindsay Fischer, Christopher Fleming, Peter Frame, Lauren Hauser, Melissa Hayden, Arch Higgins, Nicole Hlinka, Norma Hoffman, Darla

Hoover, Kipling Houston, Ben Huys, Zippora Karz, Allegra Kent, Robert LaFosse, Deni Lamont, Sean Lavery, Nicole Loizides, Cassandra Macino, Miriam Mahdaviani, Robert Maiorano, Peter Martins, Marnee Morris, Peter Naumann, Shaun O'Brien, Teresa Reyes, Kathleen Tracy, Jennifer Tinsley, Roma Sosenko, Helgi Tomasson, and Diana White.

I gratefully acknowledge and appreciate the parents and families who have generously donated their time to assist with productions of the Ohman School of Ballet and New York Dance Theater.

Finally, I wish to thank, with all my heart, my loyal cousins, the Petersons. Arne and Rose, Glenn and Barbara, Mark and Marguerite, Wayne and Karen, Amanda, Alex and Andrew, Matthew and Daniel: I could never have done any of this without you.

ABOUT THE AUTHORS

FRANK OHMAN is an internationally known dance professional who joined the New York City Ballet in 1962, where he was a soloist for twenty-two years. He appeared in leading and solo roles in the ballets of George Balanchine, Jerome Robbins, Frederic Ashton, Anthony Tudor, David Lichine, John Taras, and Jacques d'Amboise. He partnered many of the world's leading ballerinas including Maria Tallchief, Marjorie Tallchief, Melissa Hayden, Suzanne Farrell, Allegra Kent, Patricia McBride, Gelsey Kirkland, Cynthia Gregory, Carol Sumner, Kay Mazzo, and Suki Schorer. Frank is the Founder, Ballet Master, and Artistic Director of the New York Dance Theater and the Frank Ohman School of Ballet. He has been a prolific choreographer, creating over 200 original ballets, and is currently directing his talents towards teaching, choreography, and artistic direction.

EMILY BERKOWITZ received her M.A. degree in English from C.W. Post. She also possesses an M.S. degree from Hofstra University and a B.S. degree from Cornell University. Ms. Berkowitz is a versatile writer, having published articles in *Dancer*, *Confrontation Magazine*, the *Port Washington News*, and section cover stories in *Newsday*. Ms. Berkowitz has regularly attended the New York City Ballet for more than thirty years. Her extensive collection of books about ballet, with an emphasis on this company and its history, was a factor in realizing that the literature lacked a volume describing Balanchine's male friendships and brilliance as a teacher. The author is currently an educator at the Holocaust Memorial and Tolerance Center in Glen Cove, NY. She lives with her veterinarian husband, Jay, and their three dogs, in Port Washington, New York. Her son, Justin, and his wife Jessica, are newly minted Balanchine fans.

Made in the USA
Charleston, SC
20 January 2014